I0160039

Table of Contents

Special thanks to Bill Berg of www.ppsh41.com for assistance in proofreading and the lending of valuable information on the PPSh-41 weapon system.

PPSh-41
7.62x25mm
Submachine Gun

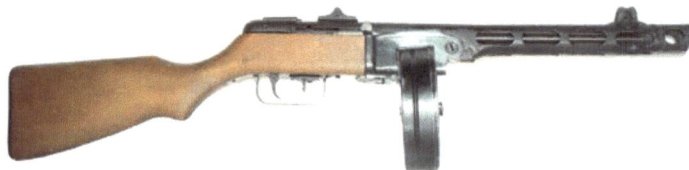

Practical Guide to the Operational Use of the PPSh-41 SubMachine Gun

By Erik Lawrence

Copyright ©2014 Erik Lawrence

Erik Lawrence
www.vig-sec.com   erik@vig-sec.com

Printed and bound in the United States of America

First printing 2007
Second Printing 2014

ISBN-10: 1-941998-05-4
ISBN-13: 978-1-941998-05-2
EBOOK – ISBN 13: 978-1-941998-24-3
LCCN: Not yet assigned

ATTENTION US MILITARY UNITS, US GOVERNMENT AGENCIES AND PROFESSIONAL ORGANIZATIONS: Quantity discounts are available on bulk purchases of this book. Special books or book excerpts can also be created to fit specific needs. For information, please contact:

Erik Lawrence
www.vig-sec.com   erik@vig-sec.com

CREDITS:
Wikipedia contributors, "Main Page," Wikipedia, The Free Encyclopedia,
http://en.wikipedia.org/w/index.php?title=Main_Page&oldid=83971314
(accessed October 7, 2006).

Firearms are potentially dangerous and must be handled responsibly by individuals. The technical information presented in this manual on the use of the PPSh-41 SubMachine Gun reflects the author's research, beliefs, and experiences. The information in this book is presented for academic study only. Neither the author nor the publisher assumes any responsibility for the use or misuse of information contained in this book.

SAFETY NOTICE
Before starting an inspection, ensure the weapon is cleared. Do not manipulate the trigger until the weapon has been cleared of all ammunition. Inspect the chamber to ensure that it is empty and no ammunition is present. Keep the weapon oriented in a safe direction when loading and handling.

AMMUNITION NOTICE- This weapon fires the 7.62x25mm (Tokarev), not the 9x19mm NATO (9mm Luger) or 9x18mm (Makarov). Firing the incorrect ammunition will damage the weapon and possibly injure the operator.

Training should be received from knowledgeable and experienced operators on this particular weapons system. Vigilant Security Services, LLC provides this training and continually perfects its instruction with up-to-date information from actual use.

www.vig-sec.com

Section 1

Introduction

The objective of this manual is to allow the reader to be able to use the Shpagin-designed PPSh-41 submachine gun (SMG) competently. The manual will give the reader background/specifications of the weapon; instructions on its operation, disassembly, and assembly; proper firing procedure; and malfunction/misfire procedures. Operator-level maintenance will also be detailed to allow the reader to understand and become competent in the use and maintenance of the PPSh-41 SMG.

Figure 1-1 PPSh-41 Designer Georgii Shpagin

Description

The PPSh-41 became the staple of the Soviet Army soldier in the Second World War. The PPSh-41 was needed to fill in as a cheap-to-produce and mechanically simple submachine gun with a high rate of fire for close combat. The Shpagin machine pistol worked according to the principle of the blowback bolt. A select-fire mechanism allowed for semi- or full-automatic fire modes. A safety knob was installed in the retracting handle as in the PPD. Sight adjustment was graduated up to 500 m. The weapon was designed to fire in a simplistic full-automatic mode with an integrated compensator to help prevent muzzle climb during automatic fire. Shpagin fixed the stability issue of the weapon while shooting by introducing into his design an inclined muzzle brake-compensator, which is part of the barrel shroud. The weapon could be fitted with a 35-round curved stick magazine or the 71-round Suomi drum.

The fiber buffer, which takes its impacts with the withdrawal of the bolt to the rear position, also contributed to the stability of the weapon during shooting, simultaneously increasing the vitality of the receiver group and mobile parts of automation. For the protection of hands from heating of the barrel while shooting, the barrel shroud was made with oval openings for better ventilation and cooling. To increase the operating characteristics of the machine pistol, Shpagin contributed the simple design of the receiver group, which is removed upward, in contrast to PPD, where the receiver group had a back plate on a threaded connection. The high reliability of the work of this submachine gun under any, including most complex conditions, is achieved by its simplicity. It is broken down into five parts, which ensured its rapid study and mastery by Red Army soldiers.

A very reliable weapon, it fired the powerful Soviet P1 pistol cartridge 7.62 x 25mm (interchangeable with 7.63 Mauser) at a high rate of fire and with a large magazine capacity. Operation was selective, full-automatic and semi-automatic. The PPSh41 was ideally suited to the requirements and tactics employed by the Soviet and Satellite Forces.

The characteristics of the Soviet PPSH-41 SMG

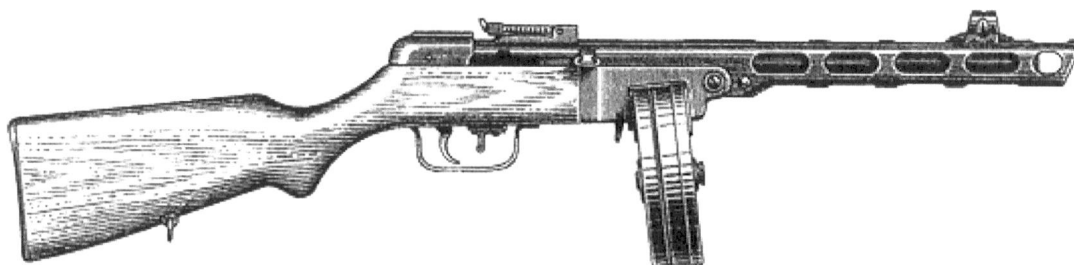

Figure 1-2 Early PPSh-41

   A. Country of Origin: USSR/Russia

   B. Military Designation: <u>P</u>istolet-<u>P</u>ulemyot <u>Sh</u>pagina obr 1941G (PPSH-41)

   C. Operation: Full- and semi-automatic fire

   D. Cartridge: 7.62x25mm Soviet Tokarev

   E. Ammunition:

      a. Type P1; 86 gr bullet, 8 gram charge (1.35" length)

         i. Muzzle Velocity: 1500 fps

      b. Type P-41; 74 gr bullet, 8 gram charge, AP/Incendiary (1.36" length)

         i. Muzzle Velocity: 1600 fps

F. Length: 33 in (838mm)

G. Barrel: 10.5 in (266mm), 4-groove, right-hand twist

H. Weight

    a. SMG: 8 lbs. (3.64kg) Unloaded

    b. Stick magazine – 35 rounds:

        i. Loaded- 1.5 lbs. (.7 kg)

        ii. Unloaded- .7 lbs (.3 kg)

    c. Drum magazine – 72 rounds:

        i. Loaded- 4 lbs. (1.8 kg)

        ii. Unloaded- 2.25 lbs (1 kg)

I. Type of Feed: 35-round detachable box or 72-round drum

J. Operating System: Blowback, open bolt

K. Rate of Fire: 900 rpm

L. Maximum Effective Range: 200 meters

Background

The PPSh-41 became the staple of the Soviet Army soldier in the Second World War. The PPSh-41 was given a need to fill as a economical-to-produce and mechanically simple submachine gun with a high rate of fire.

Designed by Georgii Shpagin, the **PPSh-41** (*Pistolet-Pulemet Sh*pagina, Russian: *Пистолет-пулемёт Шпагина*, nicknamed *Peh-peh-shah*, *Shpagin* and *Burp Gun*) was one of the most mass-produced weapons of World War II. It was designed as an inexpensive alternative to the PPD, which was expensive and time consuming to build. One of the PPSh's key cost-cutting features was the lack of any screws or bolts; all metal parts were stamped.

The inspiration for the development of the PPSh came partly from the Winter War (1939-1940) against Finland, where it was found that submachine guns were a highly effective tool for close-quarter fighting in forests or urban areas. The weapon was developed in mid-1941 and was produced in a network of factories in Moscow, with high-level local Party members made directly responsible for production targets being met. A few hundred weapons were produced in November 1941, and another 155,000 were produced over the next five months. By spring 1942, the PPSh factories were producing roughly 3,000 units a day[1].

[1] Rodric Braithwaite, *Moscow 1941: A City and its People at War*, London: Profile Books, 2006, p. 236.

In battle, the PPSh was superior: durable, low-maintenance, and able to fire at a phenomenal 900 rpm (using a rudimentary compensator to lessen muzzle climb). Over six million of these weapons were produced by war's end.

Though 35-round curved box magazines were available from 1942, the average infantryman would keep a higher-capacity drum magazine as the initial load. The drum was a copy of the Finnish M31 Suomi magazine and held 71 rounds, but in practice, misfeeding of the spring was likely to occur with more than 65 or so. The standard load was probably one drum and five or six magazines, when magazines were available; before then, it appears they would have been equipped with three drums.

Figure 1-3 German troops in WWII with the PPSh-41

The captured PPSh was in particular a favorite weapon of the Germans. Due to the similar dimensions of the Soviet 7.62x25mm and German 9mm Parabellum cartridges, the PPSh-41 was easily modified, with a 9mm barrel and a magazine-well adapter to fire from a standard 32-round MP38/40 magazine. The Wehrmacht officially adopted the converted PPSh-41 as the MP41(r); unconverted PPSh-41s were designated MP717(r).

The PPSh's only drawbacks were the difficulty of reloading, the tendency of the drums to jam (solved by the box magazines), and the high risk of accidental discharge when dropped – a common fault to all open-bolt submachine gun designs. Despite these drawbacks, the PPSh-41 was still admired by Russian soldiers for its small recoil, reliability, and lethality.

By 1945, a reported five million PPSh-41s were in circulation. Their simple manufacturing processes made sure that the weapon would find its way into the hands of the millions of Red Army soldiers waiting for them. The robust weapon would go on to turn the tide of the West Front in the favor of the Soviets and drive the German invaders back to Berlin.

Figure 1-4 PPSh-41 assembly line

PPSh-41s went on to be produced in other Soviet-supported countries as well, though their numbers were greatly diminished with the arrival of the equally important Kalashnikov Ak-47 assault rifles.

In 1942, after the signing of intergovernmental agreement with the Iranians, they transmitted entire technical documentation, necessary equipment and rigging for preparing the submachine guns PPSh on the Soviet license. During the war years, the Soviets obtained several ten thousands of PPShs of Iranian production.

Figure 1-5 PPSh-41 in the hands of Mujahadeen in Afghanistan

Since WWII, the PPSh-41 has been seen in numerous conflicts, and due to their numbers and durability, they will be used for years to come.

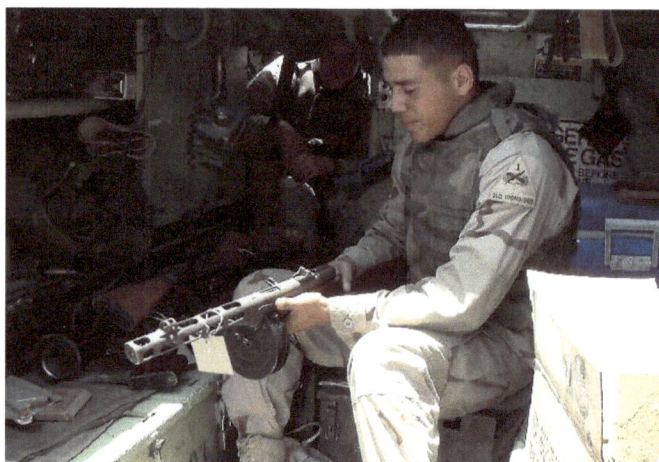

Figure 1-6 US Soldier with a captured PPSh-41, Note magazine still in the weapon, and it is tagged, hence the reason for this manual: to help the troops learn to capture and clear the PPSh safely.

Nomenclature

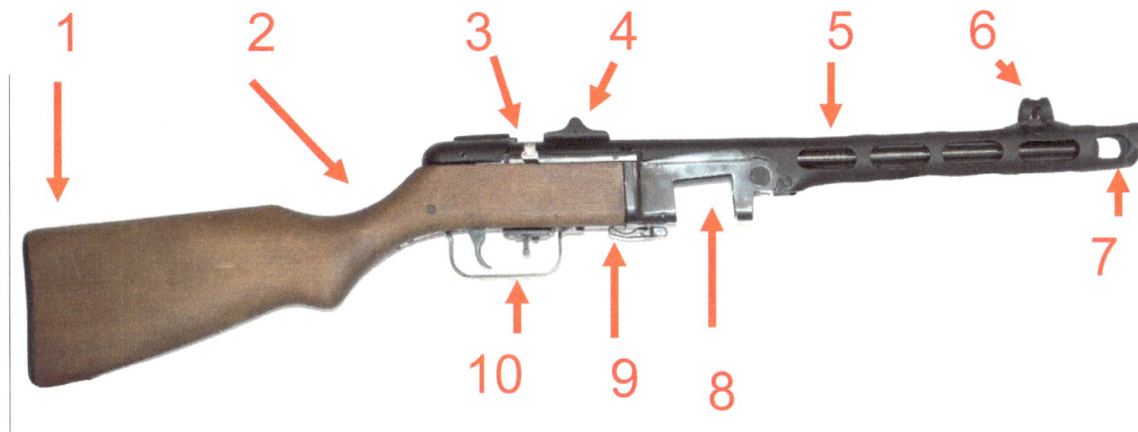

Figure 1-7 Photo of the overall PPSh-41 SMG

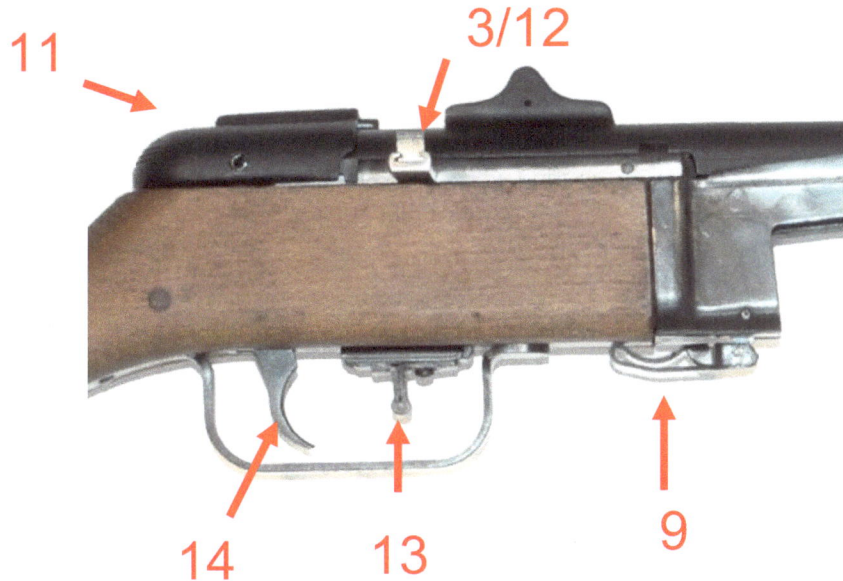

Figure 1-8 Photo of the working parts of the PPSh-41 SMG

1- Buttstock	6- Protected Front Sight	11- Receiver Catch
2- Firing Grip	7- Muzzle/Compensator	12- Safety
3- Operating Handle	8- Magazine Well	13- Selector Switch
4- Rear Sight	9- Magazine Release Lever	14- Trigger
5- Barrel Heat Shield	10- Trigger Guard	

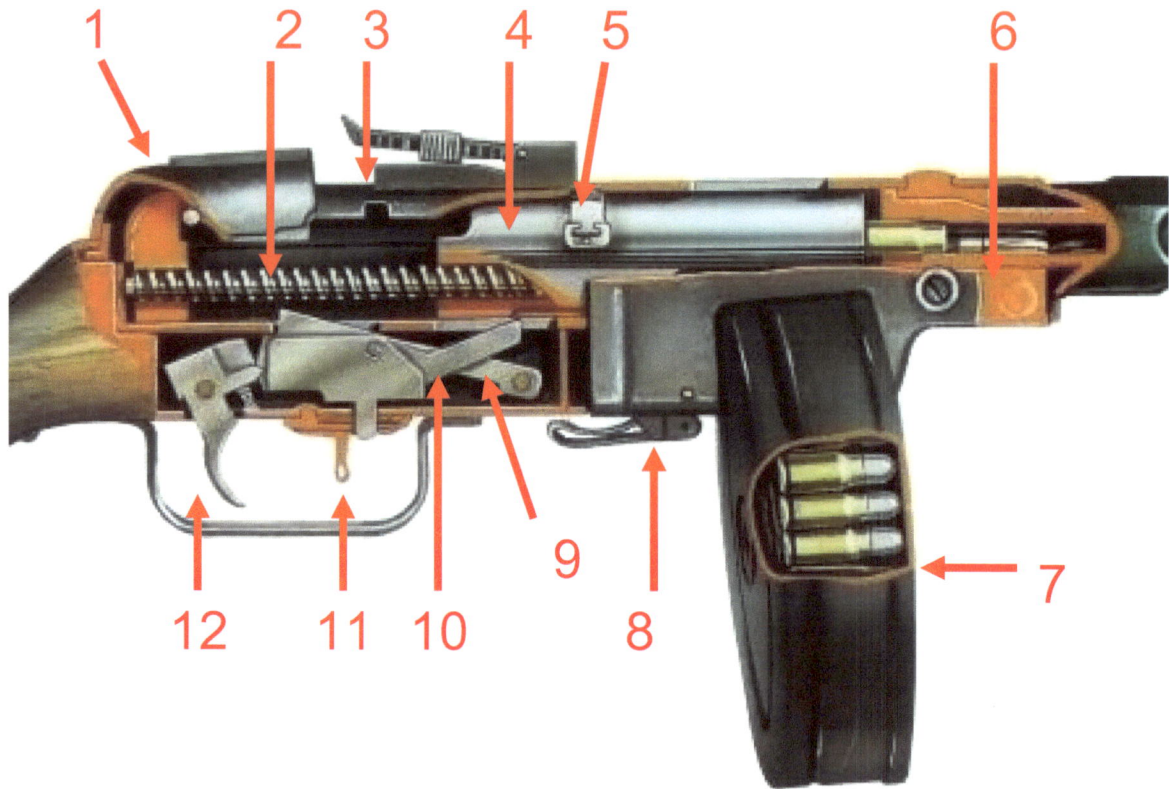

Figure 1-9 PPSh-41 cutaway showing internal parts

1- Receiver Catch	5- Safety Slide	9- Trigger Bar
2- Driving Spring Assembly	6- Trunnion	10- Interrupter
3- Safety Notch	7- Drum Magazine	11- Selector
4- Bolt	8- Magazine Catch Lever	12- Trigger

Drum Magazine Nomenclature

Figure 1-14 Drum Magazine Nomenclature

1- Drum Body	5- Stop Pin	9- Cover
2- Chutes	6- Spindle Cover	10- Hanger
3- Follower	7- Spindle Dog	11- Cover Latch
4- Mouth	8- Latch Lock	12- Magazine Spring (under spindle)

Stick Magazine Nomenclature

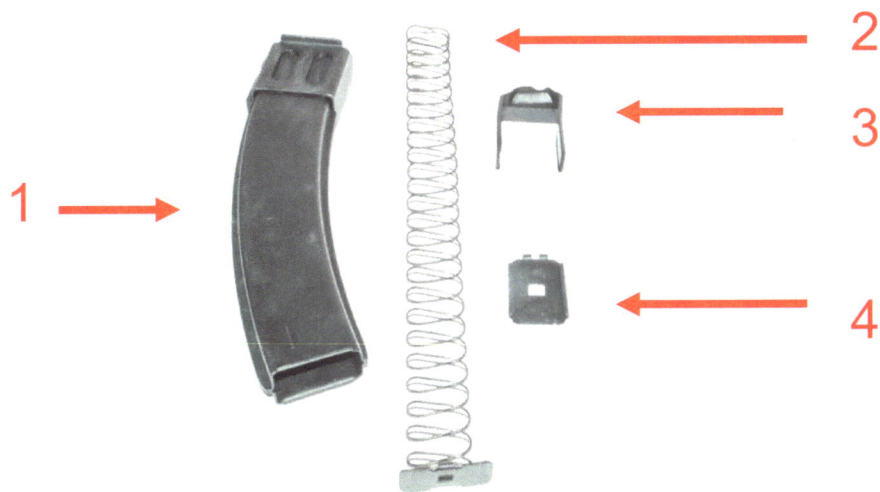

Figure1-15 Stick Magazine Nomenclature

1- Body	2- Spring	3- Follower	4- Floorplate

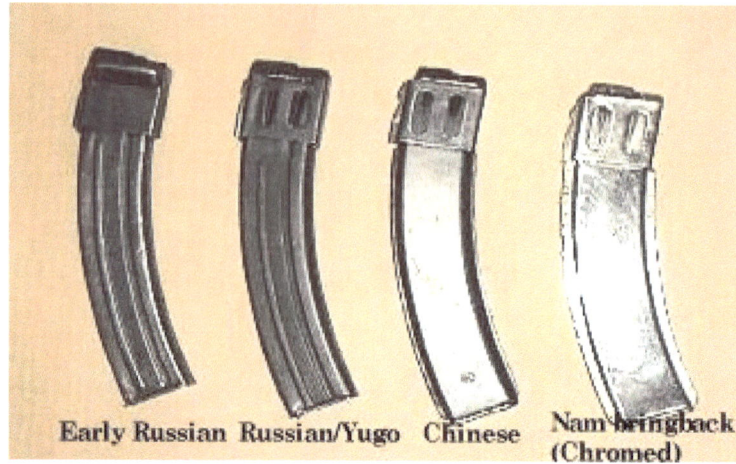

Figure 1-16 Stick magazine variants (photo from www.ppsh41.com)

Stick Magazine Loader Tool

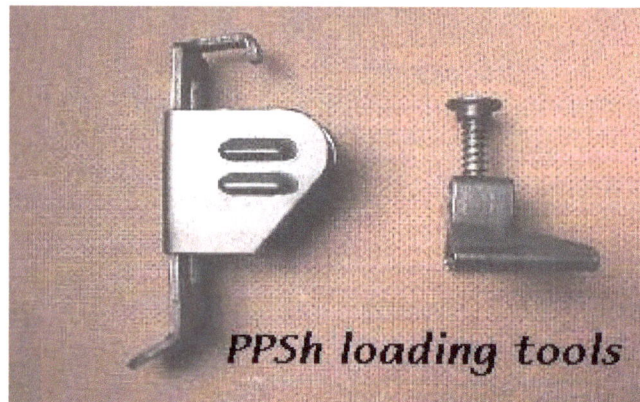

Figure 1-17 Stick magazine loading tool (photo from www.ppsh41.com)

Figure 1-18 Drum magazine pouch

Operation

The safety is on the bolt handle and is activated by sliding it into cuts or slots on the receiver cover when engaged and sliding it out when bolt operation is needed (to fire or lock the bolt into the fire rearward position).

Safety Catch and Bolt Positions

NOTE- remember the PPSh-41 is a fixed firing pin open bolt firing weapon. You must remove the source of ammunition (magazines) to clear the weapon safely. Riding the bolt forward to close the bolt on a weapon with a loaded magazine will cause the weapon to fire!

Figure 1-10 Safety not engaged in a safety notch and bolt is forward on an empty chamber

1. Empty chamber or dud round in chamber- Safety position is not engaged in a safety notch on the receiver and the bolt is fully forward on an empty chamber or dud round. This is not a storage position for either the safety or bolt.

Figure 1-11 Safety is engaged in a safety notch and bolt is not fully forward

2. Safety position is engaged in a safety notch on the receiver and the bolt is not fully forward. This is a storage position for the weapon with or with out a magazine depending on the unit standard operating procedure for the storage or carrying of the weapon.

Figure 1-12 Safety is engaged in a safety notch and bolt is retracted fully to the rear

3. Safety position is engaged in a safety notch on the receiver and the bolt is retracted fully to the rear. This is a safety/bolt position for the weapon when preparing to fire or contact is imminent. Care must be taken when carrying the PPSh-41 in this configuration as there is a danger of accidental firing due to the weapon being dropped or jarred enough to disengage the safety catch and the bolt could be spring driven forward to fire. To remove the weapon from this configuration with out firing the weapon remove the magazine and properly clear the weapon and return the safety/bolt to the safe storage configuration as noted in paragraph #2 of this section.

Figure 1-13 Safety is not engaged in a safety notch and bolt is retracted fully to the rear ready to fire

4. Safety position is not engaged in a safety notch on the receiver and the bolt is retracted fully to the rear ready to fire. This is a safety/bolt position for the weapon when actually firing. Care must be taken when carrying the PPSh-41 in this configuration as there is a danger of accidental firing due to the weapon being

dropped or jarred enough to disengage the trigger bar and the bolt could be spring driven forward to fire. To remove the weapon from this configuration after firing you must properly clear the weapon and return the safety/bolt to the safe storage configuration as noted in paragraph #2 of this section.

Mode of Fire Selector Positions

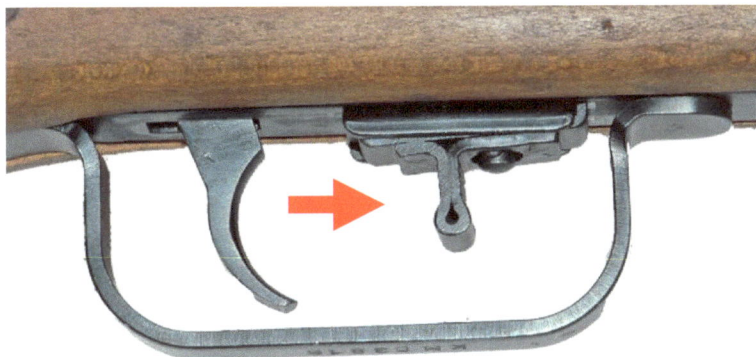

Figure 1-13 Selector is in the forward (AUTOMATIC) position

1. Selector position is fully forward for the weapon to fire in the fully automatic mode, as long as the weapon is loaded, off safe, and trigger is pulled fully to the rear the weapon will fire.

Figure 1-13 Selector is in the rearward (SINGLE SHOT) position

2. Selector position is fully to the rear for the weapon to fire in the semi automatic mode, as long as the weapon is loaded, off safe, and trigger is pulled fully to the rear and released the weapon will fire single shots.

Variants

Variations in Russian PPSh

1. Rear sights-

Figure 1-12 Early tangent sight - 50 to 500 meters (1941)

Figure 1-13 Later flip-up sight -100- and 200-meter setting (late 1942)

Soviet and Iranian flip sights have a "V" notch; the North Korean and Chinese have a diopter (small hole) rear flip sight.

2. Front sights:

- First version- Tangent rear with open front sight
- Second version- Tangent rear sight with front sight hood
- Third version- Flip rear sight with front sight hood
- Fourth version- Protected flip rear sight with front sight hood
    - Most common version

Figure 1-14 PPSh-41, early version with tangent sight

Figure 1-15 PPSh-41, later version with protected sight

3. Receiver pin: Grooved one piece -- early version. Two piece -- later version. All the WWII PPShs I have inspected that still had the original lower receiver had the solid pin and the earlier version hole (#8) in the bottom for the flat round spring (#7), which holds the grooved receiver pin in place.

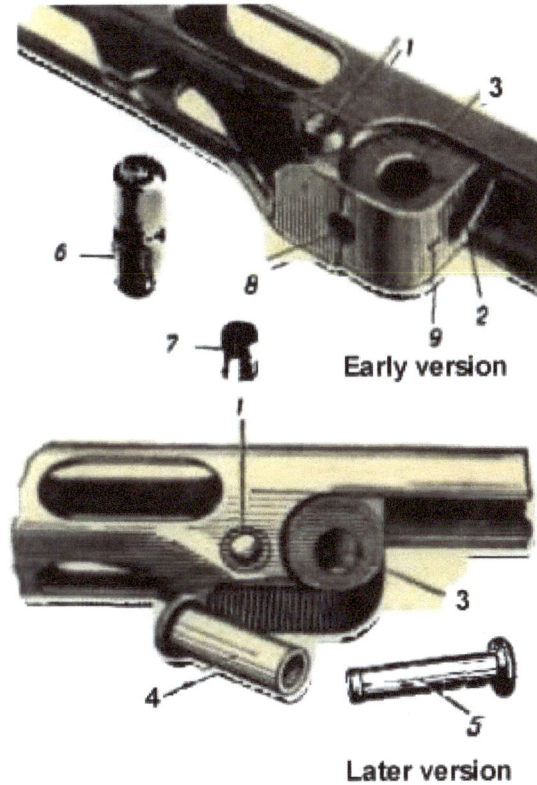

Early version

Later version
Figure 1-16 Trunnion differences

PPD-40

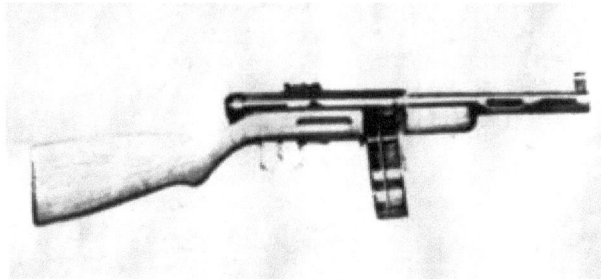

Figure 1-17 PPD-40

Caliber: 7.62x25mm TT

Type: Blowback, open bolt

Overall length: 78.8 cm/xx inches

Weight unloaded: 3.63 kg/xxx pounds

Barrel length: 27.3 cm/xxx inches

Magazine capacity: 25-round detachable box magazine or 71-round detachable drum magazine

Rate of Fire: 800 rounds per minute (rpm)

Maximum Effective Range: 160 meters

Variants: PPD-34, PPD-34/38

The **PPD-40** (*Pistolet-Pulemet Degtyarova obr 1940G*, **Russian**: *Пистолет-пулемёт Дегтярёва obr 1940*) is a submachine gun originally designed in 1934 by Vasily Degtyaryov. It was a near direct copy of the German Bergmann MP28, and it utilized a large ammunition drum, itself a copy of the Finnish M31 Suomi drum magazine. It first went into military service in 1935 as the PPD-34. In 1938 and 1940, modifications were designated PPD-34/38 and PPD-40, respectively, and introduced minor changes. Nonetheless, the PPD-40 was too complicated and expensive to mass-produce, and although it was used in action in the initial stages of World War II, it was, by the end of 1941, replaced by the superior and cheaper PPSh-41.

PPS-43

Figure 1-18 PPS-43

Caliber: 7.62x25mm TT

Type: Blow back, open bolt

Overall length:
- 82cm/32 inches stock extended
- 61cm/24 inches stock folded

Weight unloaded: 3 kg/6.5 pounds

Barrel length: 27cm/10.5 inches

Magazine capacity: 35-round detachable box magazine

Rate of Fire: 700 rounds per minute (rpm)

Maximum Effective Range: 200 meters

Variants: PPS-42

Designed by Aleksei Sudaev and first issued during the Siege of Leningrad, the **PPS-43** (**P**istolet-**P**ulemet **S**udaeva, Russian: *Пистолет-пулемёт Судаева*) was a result of further simplification of the PPSh-41, and it is often considered the best submachine gun of World War II.

It was initially produced as PPS-42, but soon after improved and re-designated PPS-43. The use of a folding stock allowed the weapon length to be reduced from 820 mm to 615 mm. This compactness made it ideal for tank crews, paratroopers, and reconnaissance units.

In technical terms, the PPS is a fully automatic weapon, based on the *simple blowback* principle, and is fired from an open bolt. The gun can be fired in full-automatic mode only. The safety catch is located in the front side of the trigger guard. The receiver and barrel shroud are made of stamped steel. The rear sight is of an L-shaped flip type and is marked for 100 and 200 meters distance; the front sight a is fixed-blade type. The barrel is equipped with a simple muzzle brake. The folding stock is made from steel and folds over the receiver. Finding too many flaws with the heavy, bulky ammunition drums used by the PPD and PPSh, the PPS was designed to utilize 35-round box magazines. This magazine would also fit the PPSh, but the PPS could not use the PPSh drum. While the weapon had a slightly reduced firing rate of 700 rounds per minute compared to the PPSh, it more than made up for this with its lighter weight, small size, and greater ease of manufacture. About 500,000 were made during WWII.

Captured PPS-43s were used by the Germans as the MP719(r). Unlike with PPSh-41, captured examples were not converted to fire 9mm Parabellum rounds. However, a slightly modified copy of PPS-43 was produced in Finland under designation m44, and it used a 9mm cartridge; 10,000 examples were produced. After the war, it was license-produced in small numbers in West Germany and Spain. It was also given to and copied by several Soviet client states.

Type 50, Chinese

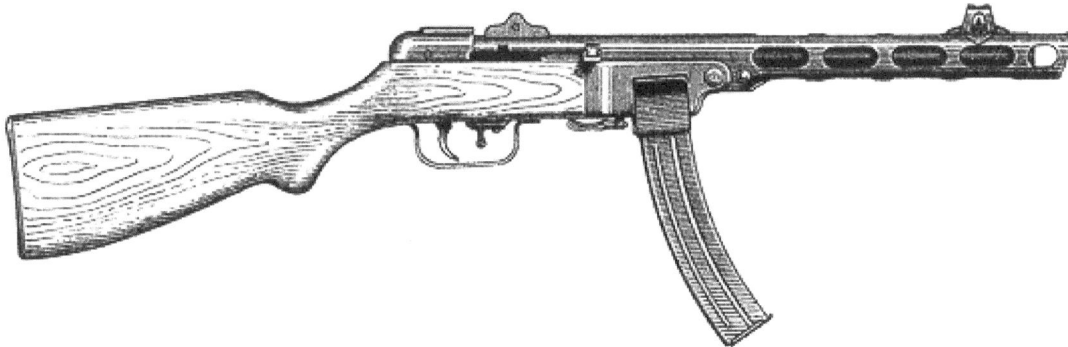

Figure 1-19 Chinese Type 50 SMG

Caliber: 7.62x25mm TT

Type: Blowback, open bolt

Overall length: 78.8 cm/xx inches

Weight unloaded: 3.63 kg/8 pounds

Barrel length: 27.3 cm/xxx inches

Magazine capacity: 35-round detachable box magazine or 71-round detachable drum magazine

Rate of Fire: 900 rounds per minute (rpm)

Maximum Effective Range: 200 meters

This model is essentially a Chinese version of the PPSh-41. The Chinese did not arm primarily with Soviet weapons until after the first year of the Korean War. At that time, they also began extensive manufacture of their own models of Soviet weapons. The above Type 50 went into production in 1950 and was one of the weapons the Chinese used when they first came into the war. With this model, the Chinese most commonly used the box magazine.

Like the PPSh41, the Type 50 had only five parts, including a black recoil-reducer pad over the end of a long spring, with a compartment in the butt for oil and cleaning brush. It was cheap, easy to maintain, very inaccurate, and had a high volume of fire.

Section 2

Maintenance

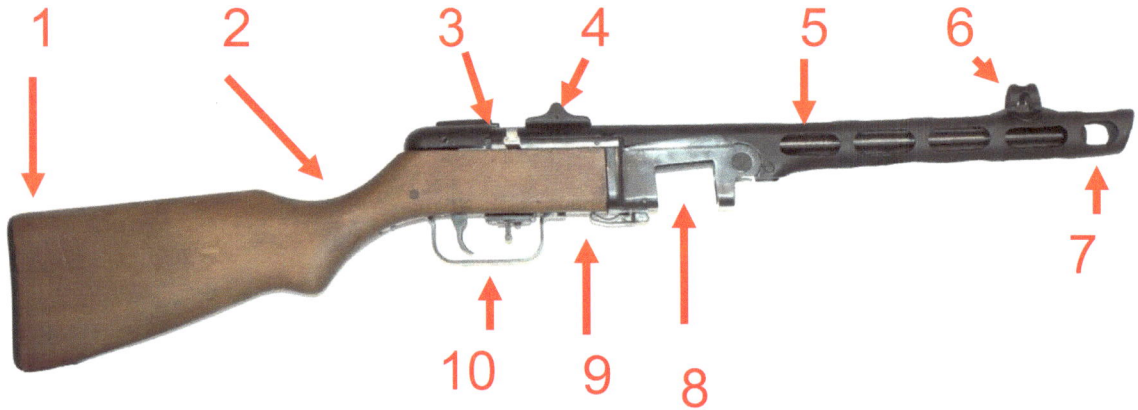

Figure 2-1 Photo of the overall PPSh-41 SMG

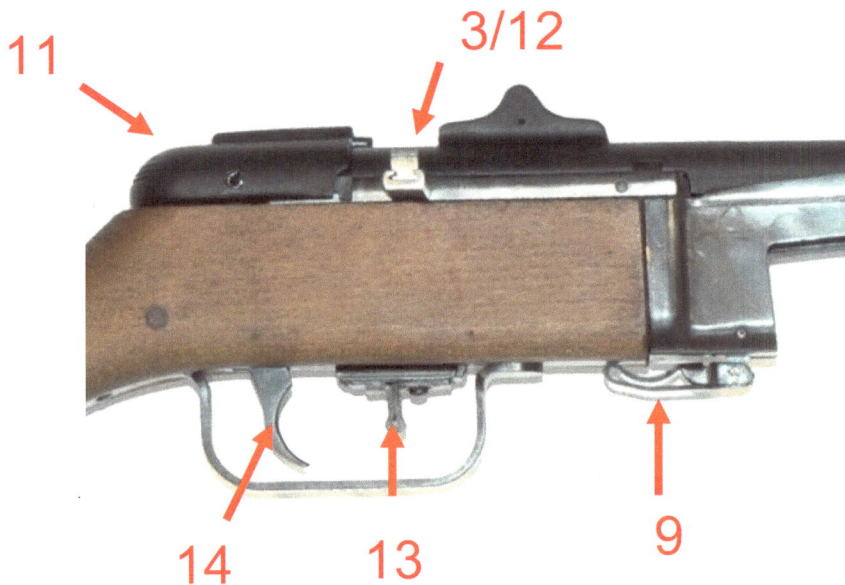

Figure 2-2 Photo of the working parts of the PPSh-41 SMG

1- Buttstock
2- Firing Grip
3- Operating Handle
4- Rear Sight
5- Barrel Heat Shield

6- Protected Front Sight
7- Muzzle/Compensator
8- Magazine Well
9- Magazine Release Lever
10- Trigger Guard

11- Receiver Catch
12- Safety
13- Selector Switch
14- Trigger

Clearing the PPSh-41 SMG

Figure 2-2a Bolt to the rear   **Figure 2-2b Bolt forward**
PPSh-41 SMG safety catch position

A. Ensure the SMG is on "SAFE," the safety catch engaged in receiver safety notches, and pointed in a safe direction.

Figure 2-3a   **Figure 2-3b**

B. Remove the magazine by rotating the magazine release lever down and towards the magazine (forward) (Figure 2-3a) and pull the magazine from the magazine well (Figure 2-3b). Place the magazine in a magazine pouch or set it down.

Figure 2-4

C. Maintain the position of the bolt with rearward pressure on the operating handle and disengage the safety catch from the receiver safety notch and pull the bolt to the rear if not already retracted (Figure 2-4).

Figure 2-5

D. Look in the ejection port to visually inspect the chamber visually to ensure there is no round in the chamber that failed to be extracted and ejected (Figure 2-5).

Figure 2-6

E. If you have ensured the magazine is removed and the chamber is clear, while holding rearward pressure on the operating handle, press the trigger and allow the bolt to move slightly forward. Once the bolt has moved forward 1/4" let go of the trigger and continue to allow the bolt to move forward under your control (Figure 2-6).

Figure 2-7 Safety catch in receiver safety notch

F. The bolt will stop its forward movement at the forward safety notch so you may engage the safety catch for storage. (Figure 2-7).

Disassembling the PPSh-41 SMG

NOTE- Place the pistol's parts on a flat, clean surface with the muzzle oriented in a safe direction.

When the operator begins to disassemble the SMG, it should be done in the following order:

Figure 2-8a Press hood

2-8b pivot the upper portion

1. Press in on the spring loaded receiver catch hood and swing the barrel down by pressing down on the forward handguard (Figures 2-8a & 2-8b).

Figure 2-9 removing the bolt assembly

2. Pull the operating handle rearward and raise up on the front of the bolt (Figure 2-9).

Figure 2-10

3. Rotate the bolt, driving spring assembly, and buffer up and out of the receiver by lifting up on the front of the bolt (Figure 2-10).

Figure 2-11 Bolt, Driving Spring Assembly and Buffer disassembled

4. Pull the driving spring assembly from the bolt and remove the buffer (Figure 2-11).

Cleaning Accessories

NOTE- on Russian oil bottles there are two containers joined. One for cleaning solvent (marked Щ) **and one for lubricant (marked H) in Cyrillic characters.**

Figure 2-12a Door closed   **Figure 2-12b Door open**
Buttplate of the buttstock with the door to the hollow cleaning kit storage area

Cleaning the PPSh-41

Figure 2-13 Photo of the weapon parts

1. Once fully dissembled into the major groups (stock and receiver, bolt, driving spring assembly and buffer) clean each individual part with a powder solvent (Figure 2-13).

2. Clean the bolt, driving spring assembly and buffer with a powder solvent and dry when completed.

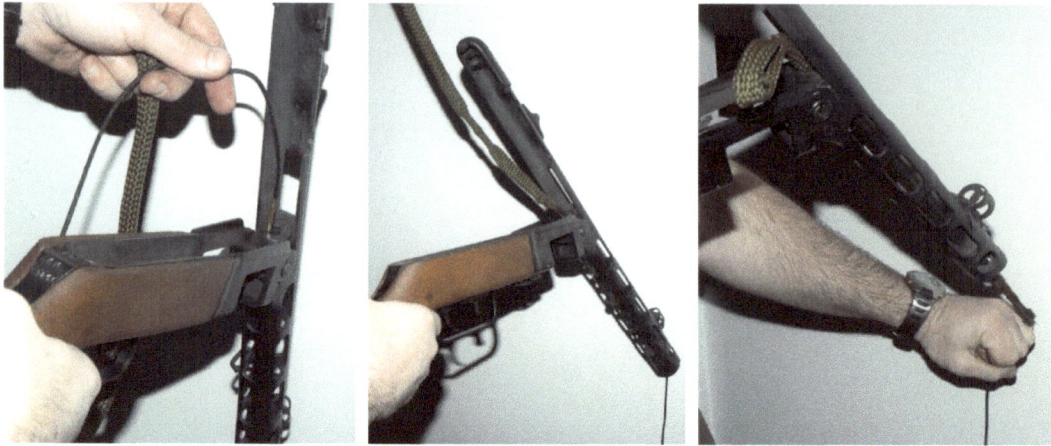

Figure 2-14a-c Photos of the Boresnake pulled through bore

3. Clean the barrel with the cleaning rods that are stored in the hollow section of the buttstock. Use solvent lubricated brass brushes to break up carbon in the bore, and then use a solvent covered patch to push the carbon out then dry patch until clean. The bores are chromed lined so they clean up easily. A bore snake is a great bore-cleaning product to do this as the barrel is clean with one pass of the bore snake. Bore snake for the 7.62 caliber is item number VSS-240115.

Figure 2-15
Photos of the muzzle and compensator

4. Cleaning of the exterior of the muzzle and compensator is required as corrosive ammo can greatly affect it due to the fact it is not chromed. Copious amounts of powder solvent and time to allow it to breakdown the carbon is suggested. Once broken down wipe until clean (Figure 2-15).

5. Once all parts are cleaned they should be inspected for damage. Points to inspect is the condition of the front and rear sights, fixed firing pin, driving spring assembly, buffer and overall condition of all internal parts.

6. Prior to reassembly of the SMG a light coat of protective oil should be applied to all metal surfaces. Grease should be lightly applied to all the metal surfaces that make contact in the operation of the weapon.

Dissembling the Stick Magazine

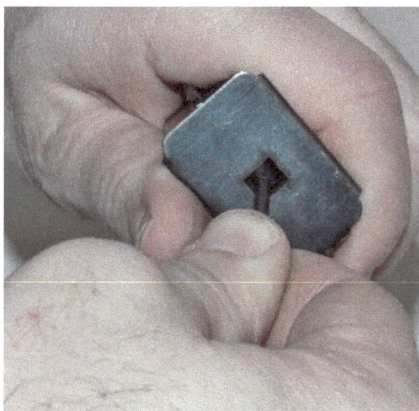

Figure 2-16a Depress floorplate lock

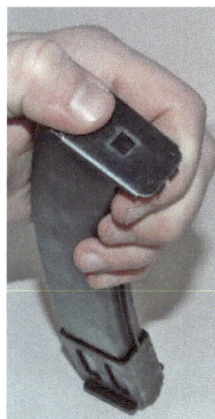

Figure 2-16b Remove floorplate

1. Use a pointed object to depress the retaining plate through the floor plate and start to slide the floor plate to the rear. The older, dirtier, and/or rusty the magazine is, the harder this step will be to do. Be careful not to slide the floor plate fully off until you are ready to apply pressure to the retainer plate, as it is under spring tension (Figures 2-16a and 2-16b).

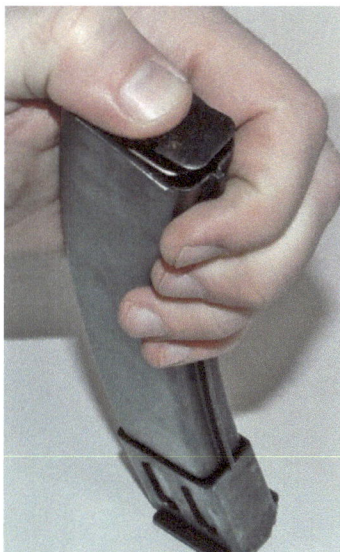

Figure 2-17a Photo of

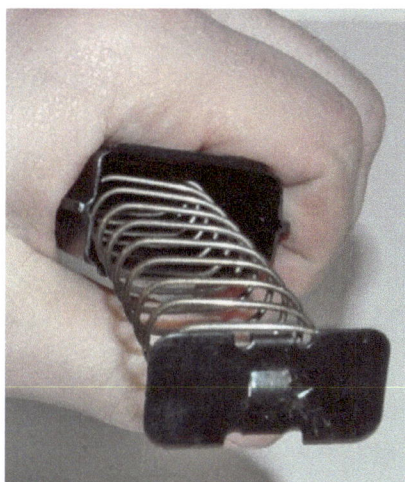

Figure 2-17b Photo of

2. Once you have the floor plate started, use your thumb to hold the retainer plate and remove the floor plate fully. Now you can release the spring tension in a

controlled manner and remove the spring and follower from the magazine body. The follower and retaining plate can be removed from the spring if needed for thorough cleaning (Figures 2-17a and 2-17b).

NOTE- It is very important to clean the inside of the magazine body and the outside of the follower. Keep the magazine as dry as possible but lightly coated with a protectant to prevent rusting.

3. To reassemble, just reverse the process.

Reassembling the PPSh-41 SMG

Figure 2-18

1. Insert the driving spring assembly into the bolt and place the buffer, flat side toward the buffer, over the spring (Figure 2-18).

Figure 2-19

2. Place the tapered end of the driving spring assembly into the hole in the rear of the bolt (Figure 2-19).

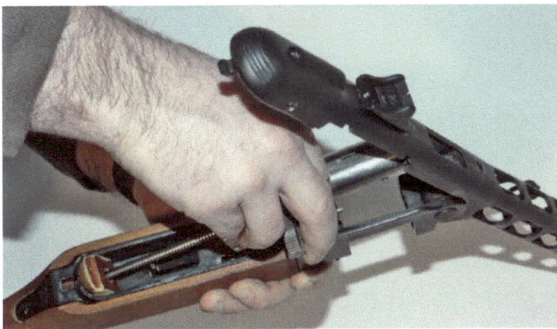

Figure 2-20a

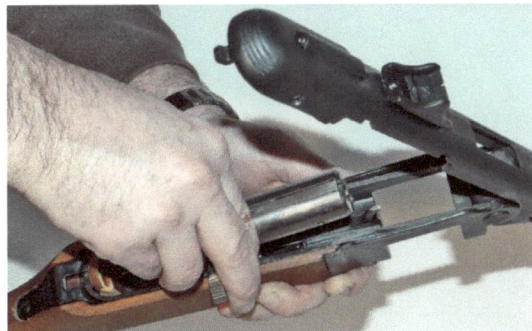

Figure 2-20b

3. Place the buffer at the rear of the receiver (Figure 2-20a) and pull the bolt back to swing it down into position in the receiver (Figure 2-20b).

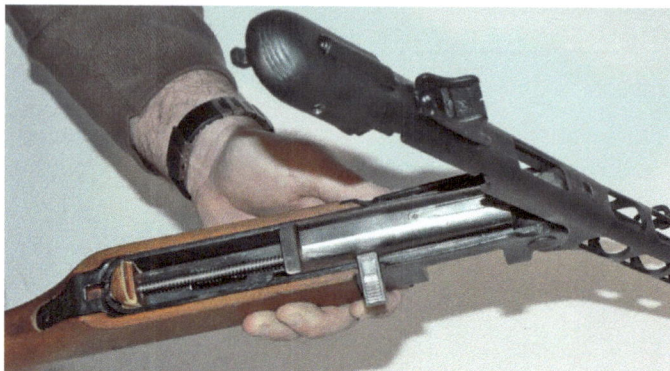

Figure 2-21

4. Once the bolt assembly is in the receiver channel allow the spring to push the bolt forward while under your control, do not slam (Figures 2-21).

Figure 2-22

5. Rotate the barrel up to close the receiver until the receiver catch hood engages, pressing in the hood to fully close. The bolt will need retracted slightly to allow the operating handle to fit into the safety notch to allow it to fully shut and lock.

Performing a Function Check on the PPSh-41 SMG

NOTE- Ensure there is no magazine in the weapon; clear prior to performing a function check.

    A. Insure the safety catch is not pushed in on the operating handle.

    B. Pull the operating handle fully rearward and release it.

    C. Push in on safety catch (SAFE) on the operating handle.

    D. Press trigger. The bolt should not go forward.

    E. Push selector to the rear (SEMI-AUTOMATIC).

    F. Pull out on safety catch.

G. Press trigger. The bolt should go forward.

H. Push selector forward (AUTOMATIC).

I. Maintain pressure on the trigger, and pull the operating handle fully rearward, and release it. The bolt should go forward.

Section 3

Operation and Function

Background on the PPSh-41 Drum Magazine

The co-designer of the Finnish KP/-31 Submachine Gun Lieutenant Y. Koskinen continued his independent work after the dissolution of Konepistooli Oy. He did no more firearm designs but concentrated instead on other equipment related to them. The Finnish 70-round drum for the KP/-31 was his innovation, and it proved to be the most succesful magazine of the Suomi submachine gun, both before and during World War II and until the mid-fifties.

Lt. Koskinen introduced his magazine in 1935. On January 28, 1936, Tikkakoski Oy received an order from the Finnish Army Ordnance Department for 8000 drums m/Koskinen. Follow-up orders were for 20,000 drums in April 1936 and for 21,000 magazines in January 1937, a sufficient quantity for the 4000 KP/-31s used during the Winter War.

The 70-round drum was, if a somewhat overly simplified description is allowed, a combination of two 40-round magazines mounted together in concentric fashion. There are, of course, some refinements over the original construction. The cartridge rows are no longer staggered, and the cover or lid of the 70-round drum is on the front face of the magazine. When filling the feed grooves, it is now possible to place the cartridges standing on their flat ends, thus preventing the "domino effect" from toppling with less effort. The 70-round drum has a "phonograph mainspring" like the 40-round sissilipas, but it is possible to wind it for almost two complete rotations clockwise. Each rotation is divided to four "clicks" of the ratchet. Partial filling of the drum, if necessary, is therefore easy to do, and thus the feed spring is protected from weakening. A feed-paw, actuated by a spring capsule (similar to one from a "His Master's Voice" phonograph), pushes the inner cartridge groove empty from cartridges.

If more than 35 cartridges are loaded into the magazine, these are placed in the outer feed groove. The inner groove is fastened on a rotating feed-plate. A steel clip, projecting outward from the plate, pushes cartridges from the outer groove to the lips of magazine and stops the rotation of the feed-plate when the outer groove is empty. The remaining 35 cartridges now start to flow into the gun through the feeding lips.

Imitation is the highest form of flattery: The Russians showed their respect of LT Koskinen by adopting a detailed copy of his remarkable innovation during the Winter War and the Russian Great Patriotic War. Millions and millions of 70-round drums were made in Soviet Russia and later in Red China and European Communist Block countries for copies of the Pulemyot Pistolyet Shpagina model 1941 submachine gun. Not too many users of these guns knew that the origin of the magazine in their tool of destruction was Finnish, not Russian.

Loading the PPSh-41 Drum Magazine

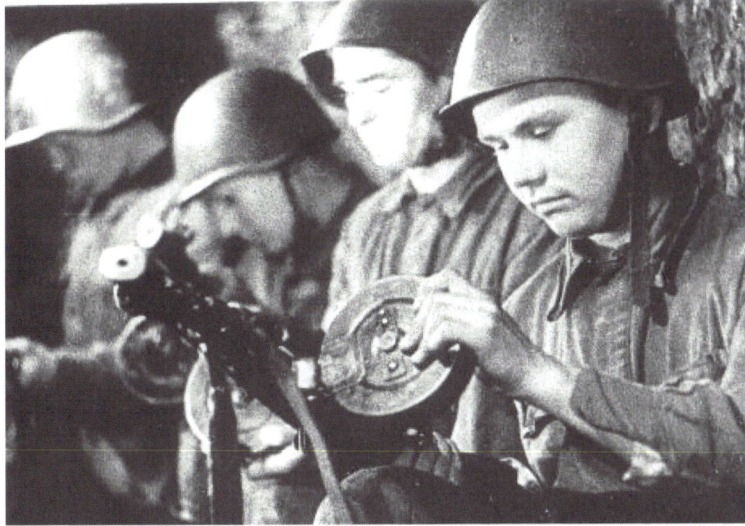

Figure 3-1 Red Army soldiers inserting drum magazines

NOTE- Ensure you have 7.62 x 25mm Tokarev ammunition. Inspect it for uniformity, cleanliness, and serviceability. Check all cartridges for undented primers and only use issued ammunition.

1. Remove the cover

Figure 3-2

A. Holding the magazine in the non-dominant hand, press the magazine latch knob upward from the bottom with the middle finger, and with the thumb of the dominant hand, rotate the cover latch approximately 90 degrees (Figure 3-2);

Figure 3-3

B. Holding the magazine in the non-dominant hand, as shown in Figure 3-3, remove the cover with the dominant hand.

Figure 3-4a Follower into inner channel

Figure 3-4b Volute Chamber must be against stop pin

2. Tighten the magazine spring:

Take the magazine in the non-dominant hand, and with the fingers of the dominant hand, grasp the dogs of the drum and tighten the spring by rotating the drum counter-clockwise. You should hear **eight** audible clicks during this process (Figure 3-4a). If the Volute Chamber is not rotated fully clockwise for the chamber stop pin is the against the drum body stop pin the drum will not properly load to capacity (Figure 3-4b). if you do not have enough ammunition to fully load only turn the spindle so enough room to accommodate the available rounds fill from the follower to the mouth and replace the cover and release the spring tension while doing so.

NOTE- When tightening the spring:

- Do not release the drum until you have heard the ratcheting clicks.

Figure 3-5 Follower must start in the inner channel

- Ensure that during the drum's first rotation, the follower slides through the internal course of the volute chambers, and the chambers themselves remain immobile (if this caution is not observed, the cartridges from the inner chamber will not be delivered) (Figure 3-5).

3. Load cartridges into the magazine.

Figure 3-6

Take the magazine in the non-dominant hand, tilt it slightly, and load 72 cartridges along the entire length of the inner and outer courses of the chambers. The inner groove holds 32 rounds and outer feet grooves hold 40 rounds. Ensure to not tip over a round into the channel and if so carefully right it so as not to cause a domino effect (Figure 3-6). Place the cover on the drum.

4. Installing the magazine cover and releasing the drum spring tension.

Figure 3-7 Loaded Drum Magazine

Taking the magazine in the non-dominant hand, with the dominant hand place the cover on the magazine if not previously done. Press in with the middle finger of the non-dominant hand on the magazine latch knob (if this is stiff press against a hard object on the spring loaded knob, this will release the spring tension and press the cartridges to the mouth of the magazine thus putting the cartridges under pressure of the spring. Rotate the cover latch up under the magazine spring knob.

Notes:
1. Magazines are fitted to submachine guns. Therefore, one must check the serial number on the cover and body of the magazine with the serial number on the submachine gun. If this is not practical then practice seating, unlocking and firing the separate magazines to ensure functionality.
2. If, after tightening the spring, the need arises to release it, hold the drum in the right hand and release the spring gradually by holding the dogs, one-fourth of a turn at a time.

If the spring is released all at once, the limiter gate of the volute chamber (this is a gate near the mouth of the magazine that allows the follower to pass from the inner course to the outer course) might be struck and broken or bent.

Adjusting Drum Spring Tension

If the top round in the drum takes a "nose dive" and doesn't feed, it usually means the drum spring tension is too weak. To increase the tension of the drum, make sure the drum is empty and the follower is forward all the way at the feed lips' opening. Turn the spring assembly to the left for one or two clicks. Take a screwdriver and remove the screw that holds the cylinder-shaped follower. Making sure the spring tension release button on the back side is away from any surface that might suddenly release the tension while your fingers are inside the drum, carefully turn the spring assembly to the left two underline full turns, replace the follower back in the same original position, close to the feed lip opening. Try shooting again with the drum. If feeding problems still exist, repeat the above and retry until correct tension produces flawless feeding.

Loading the PPSh-41 Stick Magazine

To load the column magazine:

1. Grasp the magazine in the non-dominant hand with the mouth upward and the lug to the left, with several cartridges in the dominant hand.

2. Holding the next cartridge by the thumb and index finger of the dominant hand on the projectile and shoulder of the case, press down on the follower with the cartridge rim, and insert the cartridge under magazine lips with pressure of the thumb on the case shoulder.

3. Pick up the next cartridge in the same manner, and placing its rim on the cartridge just inserted into the magazine, insert this cartridge under the magazine lips.

4. Continue to load 30-35 cartridges into the magazine in the same manner.

A special tool can be used to load cartridges into the column magazine (Figures 3-8a & 3-8b). This tool is fastened to the mouth of the magazine, with its opening toward the front.

When loading a magazine with this tool, position a cartridge in front of the plunger, and push the cartridge in the magazine downward by pressing on the plunger. The free cartridge can then be slid into position under the magazine lips.

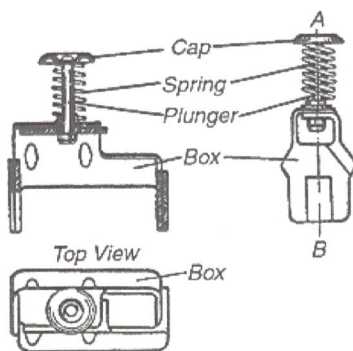

Figure 3-8a

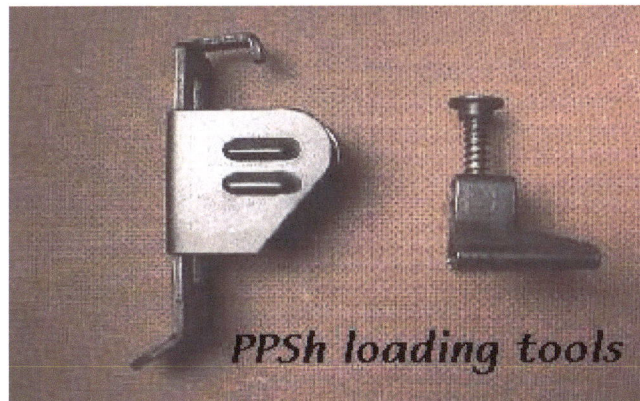

Figure 3-8b

Loading the Drum or Stick Magazine in a PPSh-41 SMG

Figure 3-9

1. With the SMG pointed in a safe direction, bolt forward with the safety engaged, magazine release lever in the closed position hold the weapon with the non dominant hand in front of the trigger guard and the drum or stick magazine in the dominant hand (Figure 3-9).

Figure 3-10

2. Place the mouth of the magazine into the magazine well of the receiver so that the magazine lugs slides in the receiver slot (Figure 3-10).

Figure 3-4a

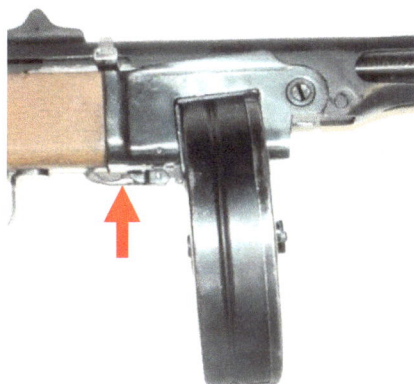

Figure 3-4b

3. Ensure the magazine locks into the receiver (Figure 3-4a) and make sure the magazine release lever is in the up (against the weapon- Figure 3-4b) position to lock the magazine in place.

Firing Positions for the PPSh-41 SMG

**Figure 3-18
Photo of standing position**

**Figure 3-19
Photo of kneeling position**

Figure 3-20 Photo of prone position

Figure 3-21 Supported barricade position

Firing the PPSh-41 SMG

Figure 3-23 PPSh-41 in combat

A. Orient downrange or towards the threat.

Figure 3-24a

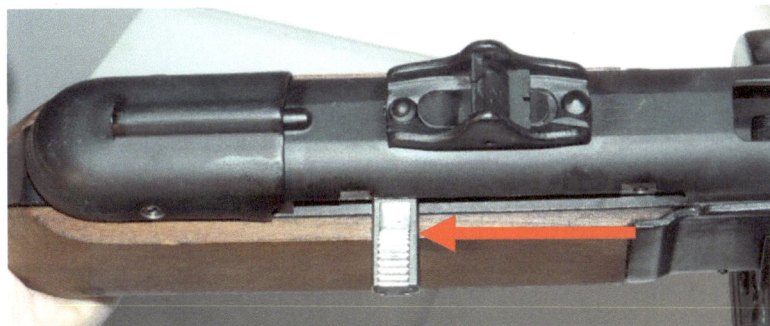

Figure 3-24b

B. If the bolt is forward and the safety engaged you must press the safety to the right to disengage (Figure 3-24a) and pull the bolt **fully** to the rear until it catches the sear (Figure 3-24b). Release the bolt and re-grip the weapon. You should set the selector to the semi or full-auto position prior to manipulating the safety or bolt.

Figure 3-25

C. As you orient your sights onto the target, press the trigger straight back so as not to interrupt the sight picture (Figure 3-25). As the PPSh-41 is an open bolt weapon, you will notice the movement of the bolt forward once you press the trigger; take this movement into account to maintain your sight alignment and sight picture on the target.

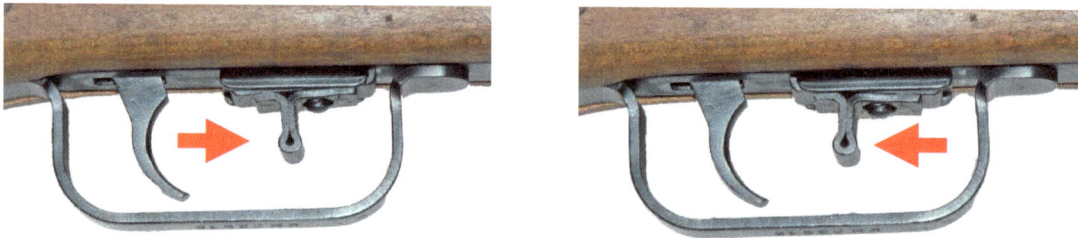

Figure 3-26a Forward (AUTOMATIC)   Figure 3-26b Rearward (SEMI-AUTOMATIC)
Selector positions

D. For singe shot engagements aim, press, and release the trigger each time as the target requires (Figure 3-26a). For full-automatic bursts, press and hold the trigger to the rear for six- to nine-round bursts and release to reacquire your sights on target (Figure 3-26b). Continue to burst fire as the target requires.

Figure 3-27 safety ON position

E. When you have completed firing the SMG, place the safety slide into the "**SAFE**" (in) position (Figure 3-27).

Figure 3-28 Safety FIRE position

F. To reengage a target from this configuration, press the safety slider to the right, align the sights, and press the trigger for the required type of engagement (Figure 3-28).

Figure 3-29 Bolt forward position

G. You will notice upon firing your last cartridge that the bolt will not return to the rear and will remain forward. Included in the malfunction section of this manual will be is remedial action for failure-to-fire malfunctions due to an empty weapon or dud cartridges (Figure 3-29).

H. Once firing is completed, clear the weapon as previously detailed in Chapter 2.

Zeroing the PPSh-41

Zero procedure: Attempt to do this on a known distance range on a windless day from a solid bench rest.

Figure 3-30a 100 Meter sight setting   **Figure 3-30b 200 Meter sight setting**
Photos of the rear sight and protective sight wings

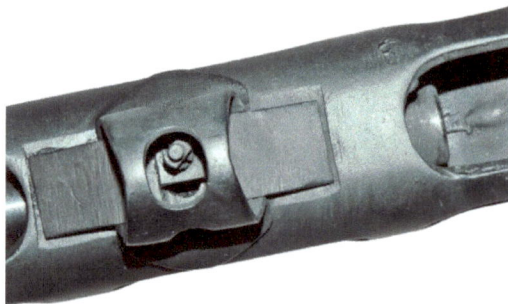

Figure 3-31a Top View   **Figure 3-31b Side View**
Photos of the front sight and protective sight hood

Sight adjustments are made to the front sight of the PPSh-41 (Figures 3-31a & 3-31b).

The front sight consists of a rotating sight post. The front sight will allow you to adjust for elevation by rotating the front sight pin up or down. Note: If you wish to move your point of impact up, then you must rotate the sight down. If you wish your point of impact to go down, you must rotate the front-sight pin up. If you wish to change your windage, then you must drift the windage slide in the opposite direction desired. In general, any changes you make in your front sight must be made in the opposite direction. The standard Soviet front-sight tool can be used for elevation correction, but a hammer and punch should be utilized for windage changes.

Establish a Zero

- Distance to target should be 50 meters, and the sight should be set on "20" (for 200 meters).
- Target should be 12 inches/ 30 cm high by 8 inches/ 20 cm, roughly a piece of letter-sized paper on a target silhouette.
- From a bench or prone position with sandbags for support, carefully aim and fire four round bursts. Ensure proper sight alignment and sight picture and a straight back press of the trigger. If your shots are not striking the point-of-aim, then adjust your sights.
- To raise the next shot group, rotate the front-sight post in the down direction (clockwise).
- To lower the next shot group, rotate the front-sight post in the up direction (counter-clockwise).
- To move the next shot group left, drift the front sight to the right.
- To move the next shot group right, drift the front sight to the left.
- Continue to fire four-shot bursts and adjust the sights until you have at least a three out of four hits on the piece of paper.
- Once this step is done, the SMG is now combat-zeroed. Remember: All shots taken closer than 50 meters will be slightly high but not by more than 3" at extremely close ranges.
- Also remember the PPSh-41 was designed to be a submachine gun, not a sniper rifle; group sizes will be looser than rifles.

Section 4

Performance Problems

Malfunction and Immediate Action Procedures

Malfunctions are usually preventable through good practices, but they may still occur out of the blue from time to time. Of course, you hope it is on the practice range, but you should treat each one as if you are in a life-or-death situation. Practicing proper and effective corrective actions will allow you to be more confident in your pistol handling. In stressful situations, you can become much more stressed due to an unforeseen malfunction that is easy to correct. I have observed many shooters that perceive themselves to be experienced, but when they encounter a stovepipe, they nearly disassemble the pistol rather than sweep it out and continue.

Malfunction drills must fix the problem 100% of the time (excluding a weapon stoppage—broken weapon) the first time performed. You must look at the pistol and identify the problem (obviously the pistol is not functioning as you need, so you must transition to another weapon or rectify the situation). It is a non-functioning weapon at this point—fix it.

You should always practice taking a covered position to correct malfunctions with considerations on how you operate.

The following pages in this chapter describe and detail corrective actions for the various malfunctions that may be encountered.

Malfunction	Probable Cause	Corrective Action
Cartridge stuck at chamber opening. Cartridge unfired. Bolt not fully forward. Cartridge not in chamber.	1. Magazine lips bent.	*Do not close bolt. Lock bolt back in rearward position. Remove magazine.*
	2. Recoil spring weak.	1. If unfired round was at an angle to the chamber opening, compare top round angle to that of top round in a good functioning magazine. Carefully bend the magazine feed lip(s) so both cartridge angles are identical. Reinsert and retry the previously non-functioning magazine.
	3. Magazine spring weakened.	2. If unfired round was in direct line with chamber and partially or fully chambered, then recoil spring is too weak. Replace spring.
	4. Drum spring tension needs adjustment.	
Round in chamber, unfired, light primer hit.	1. Weak recoil spring.	1. Replace recoil spring.
	2. Upper receiver bent or misaligned.	2. Have competent gunsmith bring upper receiver back to original position.
Spent shell casings not ejecting.	1. Worn or broken extractor.	1. Replace extractor.
	2. Cartridge support 'finger(s)' at bottom of bolt face broken.	2. Replace or re-weld bolt.
	3. Bent, worn or broken ejector.	3. Repair or replace ejector.
	4. Weak reloads.	4. If using reloads, make sure they are hot enough to eject shell at least 3 feet o 4 feet upward.
	5. Receiver bowed.	5. *(From Brett):* "My gun was not ejecting spent cases all the time and I found that the receiver was bowed from the chamber end of the barrel to the locking latch in the rear. The amount of bow was a little more than 1/8" and was letting the bolt ride too high in the receiver, missing the ejector on occasion. Made a jig in my shop to bring the receiver back to original shape and now the gun runs like a champ!"
Fires round(s) after trigger released.	1. Upper receiver raised slightly.	1. Only takes about 1/16" to 1/8" extra height between upper receiver and lower receiver for bolt to 'jump' over sear. Test by holding or taping down upper receiver and shooting weapon. If this cures the problem, then place spacer between upper receiver and receiver locking cover.
	2. Recoil spring not correct length or strength.	2. Replace recoil spring. *(this cures a lot of functioning problems)*
	3. Worn trigger bar sear or cocking recess on bolt bottom.	3. Inspect trigger bar sear and bolt cocking recess for wear. Replace or repair as necessary
	4. Broken or weak trigger bar spring.	4. Remove and disassemble trigger group. Inspect trigger bar spring. Replace spring if broken. Replacing with too strong a spring will cause bolt to stop while firing full auto.
Round in chamber, empty shell on top causing a jam.	This usually is caused by the extractor not holding the spent shell tight enough when extracting.	Remove the leaf spring holding the extractor by pushing up on the extractor, which pushes up the spring and creates an opening. At the same time, place a small round object, through the opening, thereby holding the spring slightly higher than the top of the extractor... Next, push the spring forward and out. The extractor can now be removed upward. Clean the extractor and with a small pick, clean the grooves in which the extractor moves. Put back together and check the extractor tension by placing a fired shell in the bolt face and see if the extractor now holds the shell firmly.

Appendix A – Ammunition Specifics

7.62x25mm Tokarev

Figure A-1 Side-by-side comparison to other cartridges
From left: .45 ACP, 7.62x25mm Tokarev, 9 mm Luger, and 9x18mm Makarov

Figure A-2 7.62x25 mm Tokarev rounds
Left: standard FMJ. Right: military armor piercing round

Figure A-3 7.63x25mm Mauser round and 7.62x25mm Tokarev round

The **7.62x25 Tokarev** cartridge is a bottle-necked pistol cartridge widely used in former Soviet and Soviet satellite states. Actual caliber of bullet is 7.85mm (.309 inches).

Design

The cartridge is basically a Soviet version of the 7.63mm Mauser. They are very similar; in fact some weapons can use both cartridges interchangeably, though this is not recommended. 7.62 Tokarev is usually much more powerful than its Mauser counterpart and can damage any firearms chambered for 7.63mm Mauser. The Czech version of this cartridge has a 25% higher pressure loading, meaning that it produces significantly more velocity and energy than other common loads and may present a danger to the user when fired from weapons not specifically designed to use it.

The Soviets produced a wide array of loadings for this cartridge for use in submachine guns. These include armor-piercing, tracer, and incendiary rounds. This cartridge has excellent penetration and can defeat lighter ballistic vests (class I and II). Although most firearms chambered in this caliber were declared obsolete and removed from military inventories, some Russian police and Special Forces units still use it for its superior penetration, rather than the more popular 9mm Makarov ammunition in current use.

Some firearms that use this round are pistols Tokarev TT-33 and Vz 52 and submachine guns PPD-40, PPSh-41, PPS-43 and K-50 m.

Reloaders have been known to custom load 7.62 x 25mm with .30 caliber sabot rounds with .22 caliber 55 grain (3.6 g) bullets. Muzzle velocities in excess of 2200 ft/s (670 m/s) have been obtained with this method. These speeds are seldom obtained with a handgun; usually, the longer barrel of a rifle is required.

Synonyms
- 7.62mm Type P
- 7.62mm Tokarev
- 7.62x25mm Tokarev
- 7.62x25mm TT
- .30 Tokarev

7.62mm cartridges, type 1930, with a regular bullets
- 7.63mm, Mauser, made in a cartridge factory in the city of Podolsk at the end of the 1920s. The prototype of the cartridge, type 1930.
- 7.62mm, type 1930, lead core and bimetallic-jacketed bullet. Cartridge case - brass.
- 7.62mm, type 1930, lead core and steel-jacketed bullet. Cartridge case - brass. WWII production.
- 7.62mm, type 1930, lead core and steel-jacketed bullet. Cartridge case - steel. WWII production.

- 7.62mm, type 1930, lead core and bimetallic-jacketed bullet. Cartridge case - bimetallic. WWII production.
- 7.62mm, type 1930, with lead core and steel jacketed bullet. Cartridge case steel, brass.
- 7.62mm, type 1930, with lead core and bimetallic jacketed bullet. Cartridge case - bimetallic. Production in the 1950s.

7.62mm cartridges, type 1930, with special bullets

- 7.62mm, type 1930 with Armor-piercing + incendiary by bullet P-41. Cartridge case - brass.
- 7.62mm, type 1930 with a tracer bullet. Cartridge case - brass. Production period of WWII.
- 7.62mm, type 1930 with a tracer bullet. Cartridge case - brass. Production end of the 40s.
- 7.62mm, type 1930 with a tracer bullet. The case - bimetallic. Produced up to the 50s.

Auxiliary cartridges

- 7.62mm, type 1930. Dummy cartridge. Made up to the end of the 1940s.
- 7.62mm, type 1930. Cartridge case - brass. Dummy cartridge. Production in the 50s.
- 7.62mm, type 1930. Cartridge case - bimetallic. Dummy cartridge. Production in the 50s.
- 7.62mm, type 1930. Technological.
- 7.62mm, type 1930. Cartridge case - brass. Blank cartridge.
- 7.62mm, type 1930. Cartridge case - bimetallic. Blank cartridge.

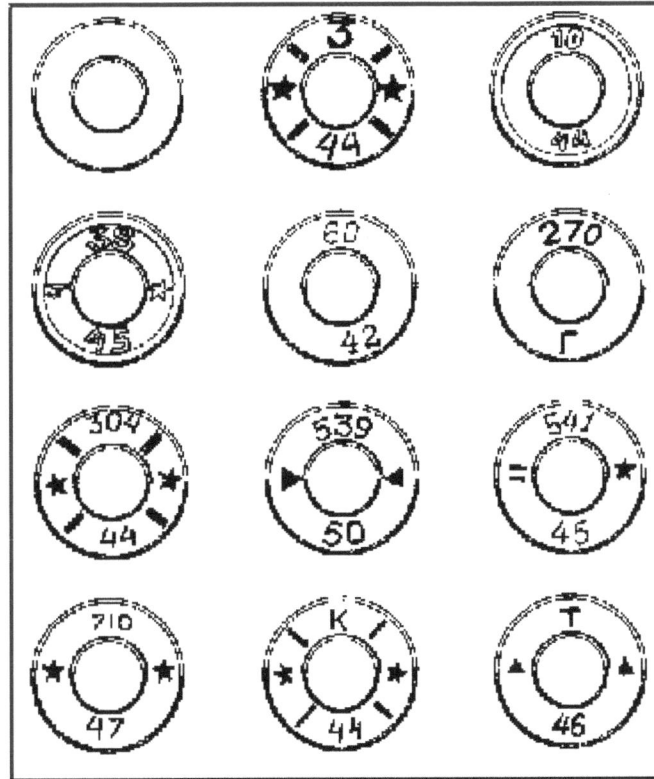

Figure A-4 Factory Head Stamps

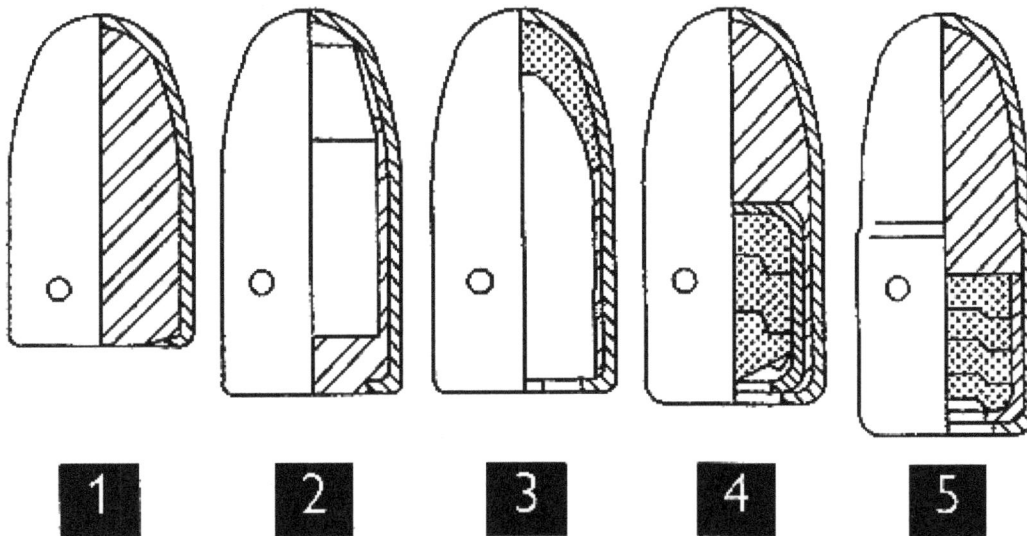

Figure A-5 Sectional View of Bullets

1. Regular bullet with the lead core "P"
2. Regular bullet with the steel core "Pst"
3. Armor-piercing + incendiary bullet "P-41"
4. Tracer bullet "PT" (production in the 1940s)
5. Tracer bullet "PT" (production in the 1950s)

At the end of the 1920s, there was a need by the Red Army for a new type of pistol. The alternative between pistols and revolvers was already settled in favor of the pistol. Together with weapon types of diverse design (starting from original models of the designers Korovin, Prilutsky, Tokarev and foreign pistols Mauser, Walther and Steyr) domestic versions of ammunition were tested. The cartridge plant in city Podolsk, at this time, made a small amount of cartridges for the pistols Browning, Mauser, Steyr, and some other models. After testing for a standard round, the Mauser cartridge, caliber 7.63mm, was selected for use in a new pistol. Most likely, the purchase had important value for the weapons of the NKVD (People's Commissariat of Internal Affairs), who had plenty of 7.63mm Mauser pistols. For standardization with the existing ammunition caliber, the cartridge was changed to 7.62mm, though the tolerances of the cartridge case and bullet practically had not changed. As for the first cartridges being a copy of the 7.63mm Mauser cartridge, the new 7.62mm ammunition received a bullet of greater diameter than the cartridge of the Nagant revolver, and more ductility of the case, thus permitting the increase of the force of ejection with automatic weapons. The bullet exterior - increase of radius/ogive had also changed, making its nose cone longer, as contrasted to the prototype. With these changes, this ammo was adopted by the Red Army under the title - "7.62mm, cartridge for pistols, type 1930."

The difficulties which arose with the development of the pistol "TT" were mirrored in the quantity of ammunition issued for it. Prior to the beginning of the Great Patriotic War, the production of cartridges for TT was limited to a rather small amount. On the cartridge cases made in this period, head stamps are absent. The cartridges were produced only with a regular lead core bullet. The bullet jacket was usually steel, a tombac plating (an alloy of copper and zinc). A powder charge weight was selected using a calculation for obtaining, at 10 meters, a muzzle velocity of 420-450 mps. It gave a bullet energy of 2070 kg/sm2, at the same distance, equal to 60 kg/m, at a mean maximum pressure, which was not superior. The mean charge weight of P-45/1 smokeless powder (porous) depending on a consignment, lag within the limits of 0.48 - 0.52 grams. This was applied to equipment and the "VP" powder (Viscose, for Pistols), who's weight oscillated from 0.48 up to 0.6 grams. The grain of the powder P-45/1, was a dark-green color in the form of a short, rather thick cylinder, whereas the grain "VP" represents a thin, long cylinder of greenish color. This powder was used in cartridges made until 1946. The production of this ammunition was sharply increased in the '40s with the beginning of the mass issuing of SMGs.

In 1941, for SMG, the cartridge with the "P-41" bullet was introduced into the inventory. The cartridge came with an armor-piercing + incendiary bullet and well-tried steel core - for defeating enemy personnel, for firing at petrol tanks, motorcycles, automobiles, and airplanes.

The "P-41" bullet, with a weight 4.3 – 5.1 grams, had a black tip with a red band.

In 1943, a cartridge with tracer bullet "PT," with a weight of 5.2 - 5.5 grams, was also produced. It gave a bright red line at distances up to 400 meters and was used for indicating targets in combat. The cupola of a bullet was green in color. The new plants, in addition, were attracted to production of cartridges with a regular bullet, and since 1942, placed a head stamp of the manufacturer and year of issue on the cartridge case. And, since 1944, when the productivity of plants reached maximum, large plants, in addition to steel, put the month of manufacturing on the cartridge. Smaller plants put the quarter date of manufacture on the cartridge case. The increase in the issue of ammunition demanded plenty of scarce materials: brass for cartridge case and bimetal for manufacturing of shell cases. On the other hand, observance of specifications was not required of rigid long-term ammunition storage - they immediately went to the regular army. Such a situation allowed materials to be partially substituted. Four plants out of eight releasing this category of ammunition had run in production cartridges with cheaper bimetallic cartridge cases, and occasionally also steel cartridge cases without a coating. There were bullets with a steel jacket without a coating or plated by brass instead of tombac. Engaging new plants in the manufacturing of cartridges, before not releasing ammunition and usage of simplified military technologies, lowered the quality of production. Later, once after termination of the Great Patriotic War, the remaining ammunition issued up to 1946 was practically completely given away to troops for practice firing or was destroyed. In the post-war time, the production quotas of ammunition were sharply reduced, many plants starting peace production. Because of reduction of deliveries of a bimetal until 1949, the cartridge was produced only with a brass cartridge case. As of 1949, there was a steel brass cartridge case, the production of which was finished by 1952, with restoration of the issue of bimetallic cartridge cases, soon completely superseding brass. At the same time, modifications were made in the design of a tracer bullet.

The last modernization of the cartridge was in 1955, when instead of the old lead-core bullet, a new one was adopted with the cheaper and solid steel core. For preservation of the former weight, the length of a bullet was increased up to 16.5 mm. Since 1951, the new bullet, step-by-step, replaced, at miscellaneous plants, production of the old bullet. Except for battle cartridges, cartridges of a secondary role were also produced. During the post-war years, blank cartridges appeared. Instead of a bullet, it had an elongated cartridge case, pressed into a "star." Dummy cartridges made prior to the beginning of the '50s, differed from battle ammo by two or three cross-sectional flutes on the cartridge case. Later, cross-sectional flutes were changed to four longitudinal. The corporations - developers of rifle weapons for the needs, produced mock-up cartridges from battle cartridges, minus the powder, left with the subsequent coating of the cartridge with nickel or cadmium.

Cartridge case with a charge and paper wad instead of a bullet was applied as a burster charge to the flame-thrower ROKS-2. (The wad and bottom of the case for difference were covered with red lacquer for differentiation.)

The gradual replacement, at the end of the 1950s, of the TT pistols with the PM and APS pistols, and also SMGs by AK-47s, at first decreased, and then, in general, eliminated the necessity for production of the 7.62x25mm cartridge. However, equipment for production was saved at plant 38 until 1989. In the 1970s and in the beginning of the 1980s, special lots of cartridges were produced, on orders of the Army, for export and for certain organizations.

For the Army, basically the color-coded reference cartridges on the bullet with the steel core for matching with the characteristics of ammunition, long time stored in warehouses, and definition of their suitability to further storage were released. For difference, the cupola of a bullet of such cartridge was colored white. In 1985, the last consignment of tracer cartridges, were probably exported. From 1965 till 1973 and 1982 - 1986, by the order of film studios, plant #38 made a significant amount of blank cartridges of miscellaneous designs. Except for the standard version, with a brass case length of 34 mm, and the so-called "universal" cartridge, with a bimetallic case length of 29 mm. This blank cartridge was used to fire from weapons using the 7.62 TT cartridge, and 9mm "Parabellum" and 9mm "Makarov."

The history of this cartridge is far from completion. Probably, it will become the basis for creation of modern types of rifles. Confirmation to that is the mention of the 7.62x25mm cartridge in the program for creation of a prospective pistol for the Russian Army. The interest in the 7.62x25mm cartridge is exhibited by the Ministry of Internal Affairs. Reasons to this are twofold. On the one hand, the widespread occurrence of a means of individual protection has considerably lowered the efficiency 9mm of the cartridge Makarov. On the other hand, in military warehouses, there are huge reserves of 7.62mm cartridges. This fact is especially significant for modern economic considerations.

*(From the Russian magazine **"MasterGun"** [МАСТЕР-РУЖЬЕ] #7/8, 1996)*

Appendix B - Ammunition Comparison

9x18mm
Makarov

9x19mm
Luger

7.62x25mm
Tokarev

.45 ACP

PISTOLS AND SUBMACHINE GUNS

Size Comparison of NATO vs. Non-Standard Ammunition

5.56x
45mm

5.45x
39mm

5.56x
45mm

7.62x
39mm

7.62x
51mm

7.62x
54R mm

12.7x
99mm

12.7x
108mm

ASSAULT RIFLES

SNIPER RIFLES & MACHINE GUNS

Appendix C - Non-Standard Ammunition Packaging & Markings

Packaging

Russian small arms cartridges are packed in sealed sheet-metal containers, with two containers per wooden crate. Older Russian production used rectangular containers of heavy gauge galvanized iron with soldered seams. Around 1959, the introduction of painted, rolled edge, rounded corner, tin plate 'sardine can' containers became the standard.

Metal and wooden crates have standardized markings that identify the contents as to caliber, functional type, cartridge case material, quantity and cartridge/powder lot data. Specialized cartridges are further identified by a color code consisting of one or two color stripes which correspond to bullet tip color. AP cartridges with tungsten carbide cores are identified by two concentric circles instead of color stripes. Russian cartridge designation, packaging and marking practices are generally followed by former Soviet-Bloc countries; each, however, has introduced some modifications in designation and marking. Russian ammunition packaging can be distinguished from Bulgarian packaging, which also carries Cyrillic markings, primarily by the different factory codes. The factory code on the container also appears in the headstamp of the cartridges in the container.

Steel Ammo Tins
(Sardine Cans)

Wood Ammo Crate (Case)
(Contains 2 Tins + Opener)

Cartridge quantities and weights of wooden crates

Country	Manufacturer	Caliber	Rounds /Crate	Crate Weight
Czech Rep.	Sellier and Bellot	14.5 x 114	210	53 kg.
India	OFB	14.5 x 114	60	15.5 kg.
Russia	Unknown	14.5 x 114	80	23 kg.
Bulgaria	Arsenal	12.7 x 108	200	29 kg.
Bulgaria	Arsenal	12.7 x 108	200	32 kg.
Pakistan	POF	12.7 x 108	280	42 kg.
Russia	Unknown	12.7 x 108	190	29 kg.
Russia	Novosibirsk	12.7 x 108	160	25 kg.
Bulgaria	Arsenal	7.62 x 54(R)	880	25 kg.
Czech Rep.	Sellier and Bellot	7.62 x 54(R)	800	24 kg.
Russia	Novosibirsk	7.62 x 54(R)	880	26 kg.
Russia	Novosibirsk	7.62 x 54(R)	600	21 kg.
Russia	Unknown	7.62 x 54(R)	880	26 kg.
Serbia	Prvi Partizan	7.62 x 54(R)	1,200	39 kg.
Czech Rep.	Sellier and Bellot	7.62 x 39	1,200	28 kg.
Pakistan	POF	7.62 x 39	1,750	39 kg.
Russia	Barnaul	7.62 x 39	1,320	30 kg.
Serbia	Prvi Partizan	7.62 x 39	1,260	29 kg.
Sudan	STC	7.62 x 39	1,500	28.1 kg.
Ukraine	Lugansk	7.62 x 39	1,320	30 kg.
Yugoslavia	Igman Zavod	7.62 x 39	1,260	28 kg.
Yugoslavia	Igman Zavod	7.62 x 39	1,120	27.5 kg.
Russia	Unknown	5.45 x 39	2,160	29 kg.
Ukraine	Lugansk	5.45 x 39	2,160	29 kg.

Non-Standard Ammunition tin and crate marking - diagrams

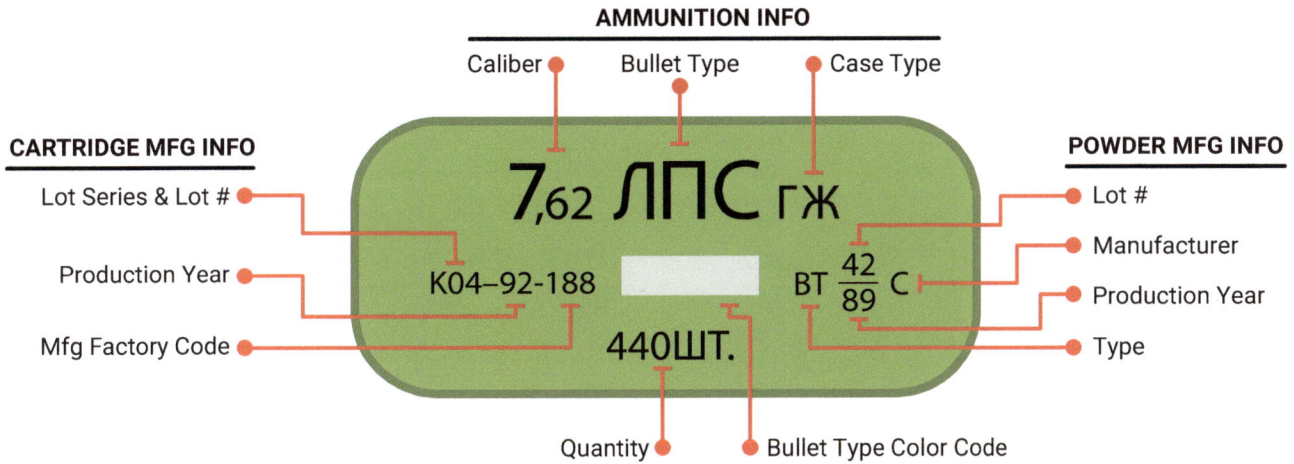

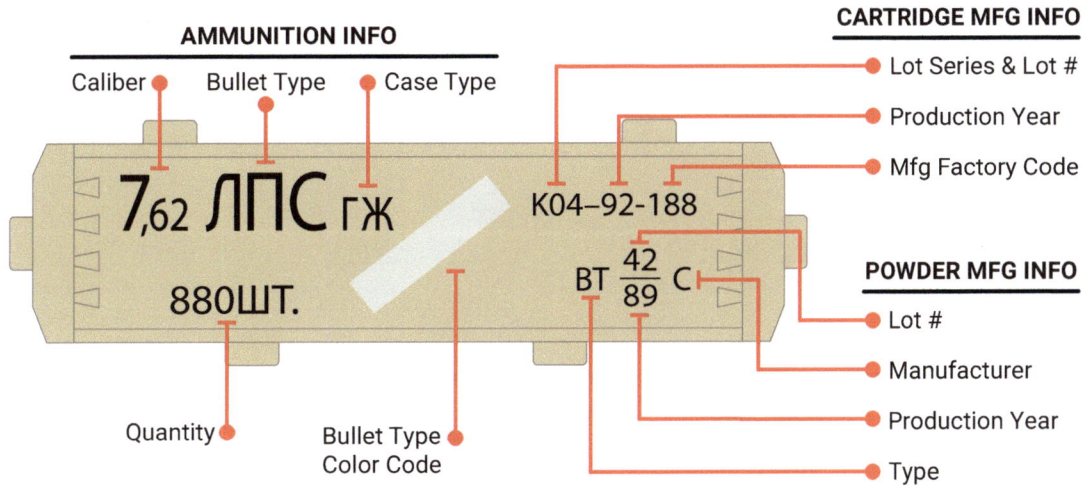

Non-Standard Ammunition tin and crate marking - Russian ammunition data

CASE TYPE MARKINGS

Mark	Meaning
ГЖ	Bimetallic case (gilding metal clad steel)
ГЛ	Brass case
ГС	Steel case

CARTRIDGE MFG FACTORY CODES

Code	Location
3	Ulyanovsk
17	Barnaul
38	Yuryuzan
60	Frunze (now Bishkek)
188	Novosibirsk
270	Voroshilovgrad (now Luhansk)
304	Lugansk
539	Tula
711	Klimovsk
T	Tula

Non-Standard Ammunition tin and crate marking - Russian ammunition data

BULLET TYPE MARKINGS

Mark	Meaning
Б Б-30 Б-32 БП	Armor-piercing
Б3	Armor-piercing incendiary
Б3Т Б3Т-44	Armor-piercing incendiary tracer
БС БС-40 БС-41	Armor-piercing with special core of tungsten carbide instead of carbon steel
БСТ	Armor-piercing with tungsten carbide core with added tracer
БТ	Armor-piercing tracer
Д	Heavy (long-range) with lead core instead of carbon steel
З ЗП	Incendiary
Л	Lightweight bullet
ЛПС	Light ball bullet with mild steel core
МДЗ	High explosive incendiary
П П-41	Spotting / ranging
ПЗ	Incendiary spotting / ranging
ПП	Enhanced penetration
ПС	Spotting / ranging with mild steel core
ПТ	Spotting / ranging tracer
СНБ	Armor-piercing sniper
Т Т-30 Т-45 Т-46	Tracer
57-У-322 57-У-323	Cartridge with higher powder charge
57-У-423	High-pressure cartridge
57-Х-322 57-Х-323 57-Х-340	Blank cartridge
57-НЕ-УЧ	Training cartridge
7Н1	Sniper bullet

BULLET TYPE COLOR CODES (Ammunition up to 14.5mm)

Color	Meaning
No color	Ball
White tip	Reference Ball
Silver tip	Light ball with steel core
Yellow tip	Heavy ball, or ball with torpedo base (on 7.62x54R)
Blue tip + white band	Short range ball 14.5x114 (only Hungarian and Czech)
Green tip + white band	Short range, tracer, (only Czech designation, only found on 7.62x39 with round nose)
Green tip	Tracer
Green tip & head-stamp or entire cartridge green	Subsonic ammunition for silencer-weapons
Red tip	Spotting charge, incendiary
Red tip + white band	Short range tracer ball 14.5x114 (only Hungarian designation)
Entire bullet red	High explosive bullet (7.62x54R after 1945)
Entire bullet red	High explosive bullet (on 12.7 and 14.5mm)
Magenta tip + red band	Armor piercing incendiary tracer
Black tip + red band	Armor piercing incendiary
Black tip + red shell	Armor piercing incendiary with tungsten carbide core
Black tip + yellow band	Armor piercing incendiary Phosphorus 12.7
Black tip	Armor piercing

** The bullet tip color codes in the table above will be the same color codes on the tins or crates, but they will be color stripes on the packaging.

Example:

CARTRIDGE
Black Tip + Red Band

TIN or CRATE
Black Stripe + Red Stripe

Appendix D - Non-Standard Weapon Identification Markings

General Identification Markings

There are various identification markings found on non-standard weapons. Typically the markings will provide some or all of the following information:
- factory name or stamp (proof mark)
- caliber & serial number
- selector lever markings/symbols
- rear sight mark/symbol

NOTE: Data tables are not all inclusive, but they cover the more common weapon manufacturers.

Selector Lever Markings on Kalashnikov Rifles

Upper/ Safe Symbol	Mid/ Full-Auto Symbol	Lower/ Semi-Auto Symbol	Country
	Д	1	Albania
	L	D	Albania
	AB	ЕД	Bulgaria
	L	D	China
	进	单	China
	30	1	Czechoslovakia
	آلی	فردی	Egypt
	D	E	Egypt
	D	E	East Germany
	∞	1	Hungary
أ	ص	م	Iraq
	련	단	North Korea
	C	P	Poland
	Z	O	Poland
S	A	R	Romania
S	FA	FF	Romania
	1	3	Romania
	ЛР	ОГОНЬ	Russia
	АВ	ОД	Russia
U	R	Ɉ	Yugo/Serbia

Rear Sight Marks on Kalashnikov Rifles

Symbol	Country
D	Albania
П	Bulgaria
D	China
N	East Germany
A	Hungary
기	North Korea
S	Poland
P	Romania
П	Russia
O	Yugo/Serbia

Non-Standard Weapon Identification Markings

Factory Stamps and Countries of Manufacture

The table of symbols below are factory stamps (proof marks) for non-standard weapons. The symbols will identify the country of manufacture of the weapon. *NOTE: This is not an all inclusive list, but it covers the more common weapon manufacturers.*

Bulgaria	Bulgaria	Bulgaria	China
China	China	China	China
Egypt	East Germany	East Germany	East Germany
East Germany	East Germany	Iraq	Iraq
North Korea	North Korea	Poland	Romania
Russia	Russia	Russia	Russia
Russia	Russia	Russia	Russia

M.70.AB2   ZASTAVA-KRAGUJEVAC

Yugoslavia/Serbia	Yugoslavia/Serbia	Yugoslavia/Serbia

Factory Marks on PPSh-41 Receivers

Russian Example

(Shield and Star) with
year of manufacture

Russian Example

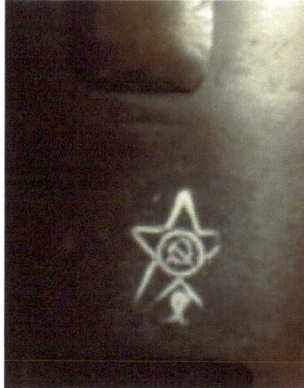

Sickle and hammer
in circle and star

Russian Example

"C" with year of
manufacture

North Korea Example

Star in double circles and
year of manufacture

Chinese Example

Chinese manufacture
mark and serial no.
with date at bottom
(2-29-50)

German Example

A WWII German
designated MP41(r)
9mm conversion of a
Russian PPSh-41 or
MP717(r) as the Ger-
mans named it.

Hungarian Example

"01" in a circle and year of
manufacture

Polish Example
"03" in a circle,
photo not available

Appendix E - Non-standard weapons theory overview

There are three key concepts to understand when manipulating non-standard weapons. These simple and logical concepts are:

1. CYCLE OF OPERATIONS
2. OPERATING SYSTEMS
3. LOCKING SYSTEMS

> Firearm design trends are shared across region, manufacturer and class of weapon and are relatively obvious to recognize.
>
> Keep in mind that firearms are essentially simple machines that harness the energy created by the fired cartridge to operate the system.

CYCLE OF OPERATIONS (COO)

The cycle of operations is a crucial basis for understanding how the weapon operates and for function/malfunction diagnosis. Each specific malfunction will correspond to a specific step or sometimes two in the COO. A failure in the system at a certain point, will by default, cause a failure of omission of all subsequent steps. (example – a failure to properly extract will manifest as a failure to eject.)

The COO will vary based on the type of operating and locking systems. Once the operating and locking systems of the weapon are known, the COO is logical.

The examples below all start from a standard reference point: the weapon is loaded, charged, placed on fire and the trigger is pulled.

'Cycle of Operations' Examples:

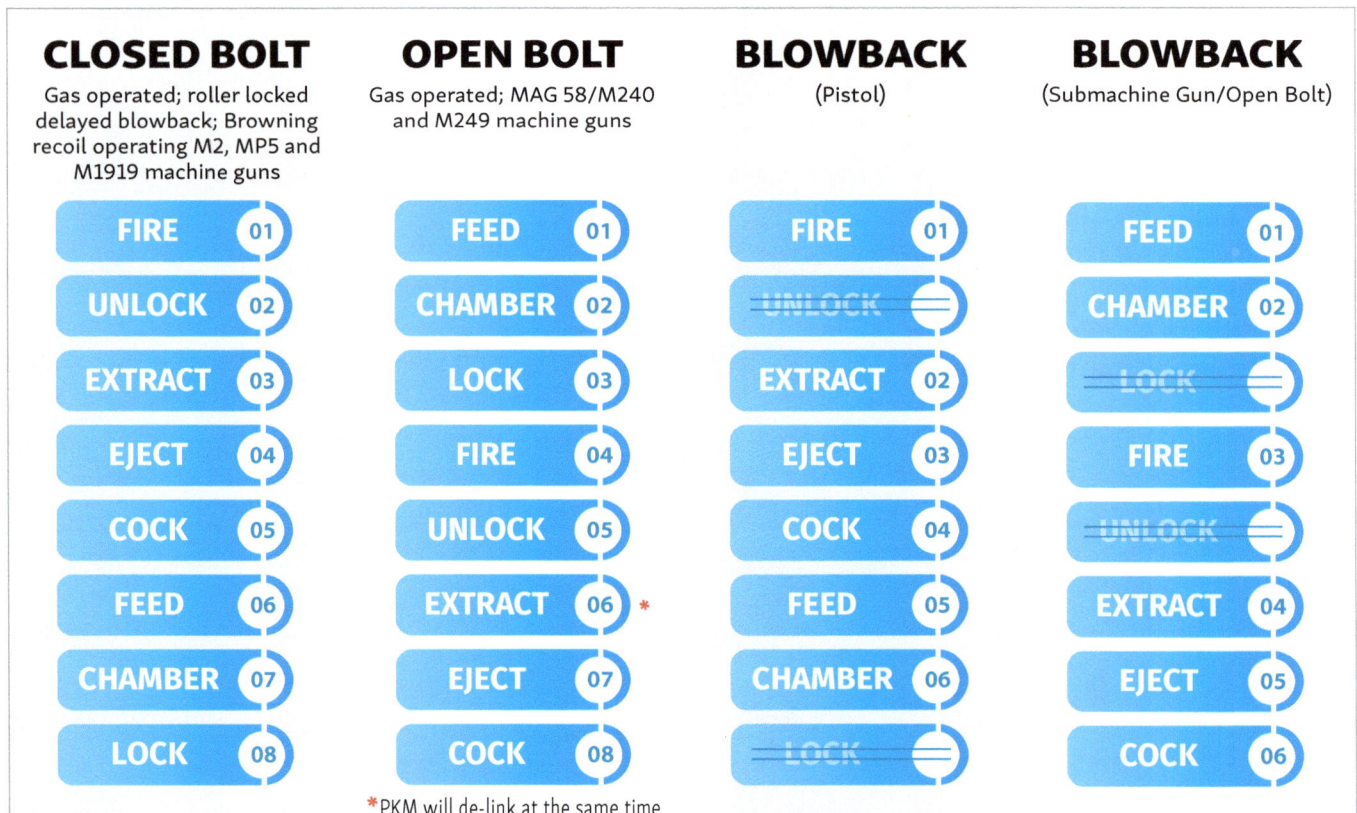

CLOSED BOLT	OPEN BOLT	BLOWBACK	BLOWBACK
Gas operated; roller locked delayed blowback; Browning recoil operating M2, MP5 and M1919 machine guns	Gas operated; MAG 58/M240 and M249 machine guns	(Pistol)	(Submachine Gun/Open Bolt)
FIRE 01	FEED 01	FIRE 01	FEED 01
UNLOCK 02	CHAMBER 02	~~UNLOCK~~	CHAMBER 02
EXTRACT 03	LOCK 03	EXTRACT 02	~~LOCK~~
EJECT 04	FIRE 04	EJECT 03	FIRE 03
COCK 05	UNLOCK 05	COCK 04	~~UNLOCK~~
FEED 06	EXTRACT 06 *	FEED 05	EXTRACT 04
CHAMBER 07	EJECT 07	CHAMBER 06	EJECT 05
LOCK 08	COCK 08	~~LOCK~~	COCK 06

*PKM will de-link at the same time

Non-standard weapons theory overview *(continued ...)*

⚙ **OPERATING SYSTEMS**

1. **Direct Impingement**- a type of gas operation that directs gas from a fired cartridge directly to the bolt carrier or slide assembly to cycle the action. (AR-15/M4 variants)

2. **Long-stroke piston system**- the piston is mechanically fixed to the bolt group and moves through the entire operating cycle. (AK variants)

3. **Short-stroke piston system (tappet system)**- the piston moves separately from the bolt group. It may directly push the bolt group parts as n the M1 carbine or operate through a connecting rod. (HK 416, AR180, POF, LWRC, FN FAL)

4. **Blowback**- the system of operation for self-loading firearms that obtains energy from the motion of the cartridge case as it is pushed to the rear by expanding gases created by the ignition of the propellant charge. (STEN, Makarov, M3 Grease Gun)

5. **Short recoil action**- the barrel and slide recoil only a short distance before they unlock and separate. The barrel stops quickly, and the slide continues rearward compressing the recoil spring and performing extraction, ejection and finally feeding a fresh round from the magazine in the counter recoil phase. During the last portion of its forward travel, the slide locks into the barrel and pushes the barrel back into battery. *(This is found in most handguns chambered for 9x19mm Parabellum or greater caliber. Smaller calibers, 9x18mm Makarov and below, generally use the blowback method of operation due to lower chamber pressure and associated simplicity of design.)

6. **Roller-locked, delayed-blowback**- when the bolt is closed, the rollers carried in the bolt are wedged into the receiver recesses. On firing, the rollers must be forced out of the recesses at great mechanical disadvantage, delaying the opening of the bolt, even with full power 7.62mm NATO (.308 Winchester) rifle cartridges used in the G3/HK 91 (G3, HK 91, HK 93, HK 53, MP5 variants)

7. **Inertia operated systems**- the bolt body is separated from the locked bolt body to remain stationary while the recoiling gun and locked bolt head moves rearward. This movement compresses the spring between the bolt head and bolt body, storing the energy required to cycle the action. Benelli shotguns.

Non-standard weapons theory overview *(continued ...)*

LOCKING SYSTEMS

1. **None** - all blowback pistols and some submachine guns – (STEN, UZI, M3 Grease Gun, Makarov, and CZ 82)

2. **Roller** - (HK variants, MG3, MG34, MG 42 and CZ 52)

3. **Rotating bolt** - (AK, Stoner, M60, and M249)

4. **Tilting bolt** - (SKS, FN FAL and MAG 58/M240)

5. **Tilting barrel** - (Tokarev TT33, Sig variants, M1911 variants and Glock variants)

6. **Rotating barrel** - (MAB P15, Colt All American 2000, and Beretta 8000)

7. **Locking flaps** - (RPD, DP/DPM and DShK)

8. **Falling locking block** - (P38, M9, and VZ58)

Function check
Checking the mechanical function of a weapon by replicating, without ammunition, the firing modes from the lowest rate of fire (SAFE if applicable) to the highest in a progressive sequence (not by selector location). The parts checked are the safety/safeties, sear and disconnector.

M4A1
1. Ensure the rifle is clear
2. Charge and place the weapon on SAFE
3. Attempt to fire (weapons should not FIRE, safety is functioning)
4. Place the weapon on SEMI, pull the trigger and hold it to the rear (hammer should fall, trigger/sear functioning)
5. Maintain the trigger to the rear and cycle the bolt
6. Release the trigger and listen for a metallic click (disconnector functioning)
7. Pull the trigger again and the hammer should fall
8. Charge the weapon and place on AUTO
9. Pull the trigger and hold it to the rear then cycle the bolt more than once
10. Release the trigger and pull it again, nothing should happen (auto sear is functioning)
11. Charge the weapon then pull the trigger again and the hammer should fall
12. Function check complete

Significant visual indicators
- Any checked, knurled or serrated surface
- Any movable lever or switch
- Pins with gripping surfaces
- Index marks (two lines that need to be aligned to disassembled (CZ 75)
- Recoil spring with ends of different diameters

www.ingramcontent.com/pod-product-compliance
Lightning Source LLC
Chambersburg PA
CBHW061055090426
42742CB00002B/54